# THE PRENEGOTIATION PLANNING BOOK

# THE PRENEGOTIATION PLANNING BOOK

William F. Morrison

## JOHN WILEY & SONS

New York · Chichester · Brisbane · Toronto · Singapore

*Library of Congress Cataloging in Publication Data*

Morrison, William F. (William Fosdick), 1935-
   The prenegotiation planning book.

   Bibliography: p.
   Includes index.
   1. Negotiation in business.   I. Title.

HD58.6.M67 1985      658.4      85-9289
ISBN 0-471-82276-0

Printed in the United States of America

10  9  8  7  6  5  4  3  2  1

*The first, as it should be,
is dedicated to my
mother and father*

# Acknowledgments

The first and most important thank you must go to my wife, Carol, who gave 100 percent support to this project. Since the project was completed on personal time she had to make many sacrifices, and without her help the book never would have been completed.

Vickie Mauser, Elfi Mavronicles, Shirley Moffat, and Mary Pampena also receive a big thank you for all their typing work. They are very good secretaries and, even more important, they could understand my handwritten drafts, additions, and other changes, and many times they typed what I meant, not what they read.

Hank Calero has authored many books (see Chapter 12). He was my role model and, even more important, he pushed me to get started. The first step was the hardest and he helped me to take it. He also is a very good role model for all aspects of life.

Also, during the past 27 years I have negotiated with and taught several thousands of people. Each had an input to this book. I have learned from each of them. It is not possible to list all of their names, but to each of them—thank you for all your help. As you read this book, I am sure that you will recognize your contributions.

W.F.M.

# Contents

# THE PRENEGOTIATION PLANNING BOOK

# CHAPTER 1

# Talking for Money

I have conducted hundreds of negotiation courses and seminars in the United States and in many foreign countries. I believe that the best introduction I was ever given as a course leader will highlight the purpose of this book.

The chief executive of an organization had scheduled a five-day negotiations seminar for all of his employees who had an opportunity to negotiate for the organization. The class included buyers, sellers, and employees in marketing, customer service, industrial relations, public relations, accounts payable, and accounts receivable. It was a large class and a major percentage of the professional and management employees attended. The chief executive believed very strongly that profit, significant profit, could be made by successful negotiations. After the normal administrative details were taken care of, the chief executive told the following true story from his childhood.

"When I was about twelve years old," the chief executive said, "I had a talk with my father because my father was the laughing stock of our neighborhood. Every time he purchased something for the family he negotiated the price, quantity, and so forth. My mother refused to go shopping with him because she was too embarrassed. All of our friends knew about my father's behavior. I can remember that talk as if it happened yesterday."

ME: Dad, everyone is talking about you. Mother will not go shopping with you. I don't like people laughing at my father. Why do you try to save money by negotiating everything that you buy?

MY FATHER: Well you see son, this morning I saved as much money negotiating as I could net by working overtime on Saturday. Yes, I know that many people think I'm crazy and that they laugh at me but that's okay.

ME: Dad, why is it okay?

MY FATHER: It's okay because I love you very much. The money I save by negotiating allows me to work less overtime and spend more time with you. I love you and want to spend as much time as I can with you now because in a few years you will be grown and will move away. Son, I want you to remember one very important lesson in life. It is much easier to talk for money than it is to work for money.

"Let me repeat that: It is much easier to talk for money than it is to work for money. Today we have a person who will help us learn how to talk for money. Let me present Bill Morrison."

As you can imagine, I had the class in the palm of my hand with an introduction like that. That one statement, *It is much easier to talk for money than it is to work for money,* is the driving force behind this book: to help each reader make money by talking.

The impact of successful negotiations can be tremendous on any business organization. In another organization we completed the follow calculations.

The profit-loss statement showed the following information (rounded):

| | |
|---|---|
| Total sales | $1,009,000,000 |
| Total purchases | 311,000,000 |

| | |
|---|---|
| Employee costs | 400,000,000 |
| Total other costs | 216,000,000 |
| Total costs | 927,000,000 |
| Income before taxes | 82,000,000 |
| Income after taxes | 41,210,000 |

1.   If each salesperson in the organization had sold the products at a one percent higher price, the organization would have realized $10,090,000 more income (1% × GSB (gross sales billed) of $1,009,000,000).

2.   If each buyer in the organization had purchased every item necessary for the organization at a one percent lower price, they would have realized a savings of $3,110,000 (1% × $311,000,000).

3.   The total of a one percent better job of selling and buying would have been $13,200,000 income before taxes. At a 48 percent corporate tax rate this would be $6,864,000 income after taxes.

4.   When you compare this extra income of $6,864,000 to $41,210,000, this is a factor of almost 17 percent.

5.   In this organization a one percent better job of selling and buying negotiations would create a 17 percent increase in income after taxes.

6.   If the personnel relations department had been able to negotiate a one percent better labor contract, the savings would have been an extra $4,000,000 (1% × $400,000,000).

7.   Adding $4,000,000 to $13,200,000 results in $17,200,000 income before taxes that could have been saved by a one percent better negotiations job.

8.   This $17,200,000 equals $8,944,000 income after taxes.

9.   Combining a one percent improvement in marketing, purchasing and personnel relations, the effect is an increase of more than 22 percent income after tax.

I believe that everyone in these areas can perform at a one percent higher level and that the impact of negotiations can be realized. Remember that all of this impact will be accomplished by talking for money—not working for it. This impact can be realized *without:* (1)

the manufacturing department having to produce more products; (2) the engineering department having to design any more items; (3) the drafting department having to produce any more drawings; (4) the personnel relations department having to hire any more employees; (5) the purchasing department having to place any more orders; (6) the marketing department having to win any more orders; (7) the accounting department having to process any more paperwork; (8) the traffic department having to ship any more items, and so forth.

It is a fact that a small percentage of the work force doing a one percent better job can increase (in this organization) after-tax income by 22 percent and the rest of the organization doesn't have to do anything different. And this was based upon a 48 percent tax rate. Very few companies pay an effective tax rate of 48 percent today.

I believe that this point is so important that you should complete the following calculation for your organization:

| | | |
|---|---|---|
| GSB | | $_____ |
| Purchases | | $_____ |
| Employee costs | | $_____ |
| Income before tax | | $_____ |
| Income after tax | | $_____ |
| 1% of GSB | | $_____ |
| 1% of purchases | + | $_____ |
| 1% of employee costs | + | $_____ |
| Total negotiation impact | = | $_____ |
| Current income tax rate is at | | _____% |
| Tax rate × impact (new tax) | | $_____ |
| Income after tax increase (impact − new tax) | | $_____ |
| Current income after tax | | $_____ |
| Income increase is _____% of current income | | |

Of course if the savings could be more than one percent, the impact would be significantly higher. Armed with this data, everyone should be able to convince top management to invest in negotiations training.

The purpose of this book is to help each reader significantly affect the after-tax income of his or her organization (if it is a profit-oriented organization) or significantly reduce costs (if it is a nonprofit organization) by doing a better job of talking for money. (Also to help you do a better job in your personal negotiations.) Specifically, being better prepared to talk for money.

This book is about negotiations and specifically about planning a negotiation. Negotiations are an important part of every person's life. Each one of us must negotiate sooner or later. The more successful a negotiator we are, the more productive and successful is our life and the lives of those important to us.

Many different negotiation situations could be discussed: (1) buyer—seller; (2) management—labor; (3) husband—wife; (4) parent—child; (5) buying or selling a car; (6) buying or selling a house; (7) boss—subordinate; (8) peer—peer; (9) business—business; (10) business meetings and conferences; (11) one business function versus another function (e.g. purchasing vs engineering); (12) federal government—state government; (13) nation—nation, and (14) all meetings (since they are mostly negotiations).

Whatever the negotiation concerns, the process is the same. The points to be negotiated, strategies and tactics, and the length may vary tremendously, but the process is nevertheless the same.

The basic information for this book has been developed from 18 years in purchasing, program management, materials management, and manufacturing, during which negotiations was a number-one responsibility. It has also been developed based upon the years 1976–1984, during which my responsibility had been in industrial management training, development, and education. Negotiations is the subject I have taught the most frequently.

In writing this book, I assumed that I was teaching that part of my courses devoted to planning a negotiation. I imagined a composite student sitting across the table from me. The book is written in the same format and using the language I would use in a live seminar setting. Questions that most participants would ask have been anticipated and answered.

This book would also be a very good basic primer for a new person in either a buying, selling, industrial relations, or labor position. I expect that it will find many uses in this area. It will be useful as a text book for university and college courses in management, marketing, purchasing, general business, and negotiations.

The major purpose of the book is to provide a basic "nuts and bolts" resource on how to better plan your future negotiations. I have tried to be detailed so the book will be as useful as possible. Since it was written as if you, the reader, were sitting in a live seminar, it is time for the class to start.

# CHAPTER 2

# Negotiations Diagram and Definitions

The following diagram is a very old way of simply explaining the negotiation process, but it is still the best as far as most experts are concerned.

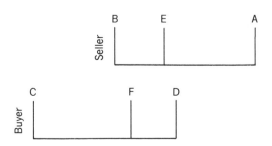

Point A is the *seller's quote* or proposal. In most cases this is the start of the negotiation process. The buyer may or may not have sent a request for quotation (RFQ), but when the seller makes a formal proposal the negotiation has started. This is true even if both sides are not yet in a room at a negotiations table.

Point B is the *seller's minimum price* below which the seller will not sell his or her product. Under no circumstances will he or she accept an order at a price less than point B.

Point C is the *buyer's initial position*. This is where the buyer starts the negotiation process. The buyer may put this in writing to the seller before actual negotiations, or the buyer may reveal this position during the early stages of the negotiation.

Point D is the *buyer's maximum price* above which the buyer will not buy. At that level the buyer may be able to use a substitute material, or the buyer may not be able to sell the end product at a profit, so the buyer doesn't need the material.

The limits of possible agreement then are points B and D. The buyer will not buy above point D, so the area from D to A is out for an agreement. The seller will not sell below point B, so the area from B to C is out for an agreement. Any agreement between the buyer and seller must be somewhere between points B and D.

Point E is the *seller's objective.*

Point F is the *buyer's objective.*

In a negotiation between two experienced negotiators of equal skill, representing principals of fairly equal power, an agreement will probably be somewhere between points E and F.

The same type of diagram can be drawn for a management-labor negotiation with labor on top (seller's position) and management on the bottom (buyer's position). Any other negotiation can be diagrammed the same way.

Negotiation can be described with the following statements:

1. Negotiation is a cooperative process for compromising known differences between two or more parties.
2. Negotiation aims at agreement.
3. Negotiation is an adversary relationship between two sides that need each other.
4. Negotiation is usually conducted by agents.
5. Agreement in negotiation is the start of a longer relationship.

**6.**  Negotiation is a psychological process.

**7.**  Negotiation involves verbal and nonverbal communications.


Looking closely at the words in each statement reveals what negotiation is all about.

*Cooperative.* This implies that both sides are willing to attempt to reach an agreement. If your attitude, or your opponent's attitude, is take it or leave it, then it is a waste of time to negotiate. Just send a letter with your position and save your valuable time.

*Process.* This implies that our conduct could be different during the actual negotiations. This is expected. Your behavior is different in many situations in life, whether it involves being with your parents, your spouse, your children, at work, at church, at a sporting event, on a golf course, and so forth. In each situation your behavior is governed to a large extent by your role and who you are with. As we will see, in the negotiations room there is acceptable behavior and conduct.

*Compromising.* This implies that each side is willing to give during the negotiation process.

*Known differences.* One of the more critical steps in the process is determining where each side "is." Determining the gap between both sides is most important, before agreement can be attempted.

*Two or more parties.* This implies that on one side of the table there can be more than one set of objectives. A very basic strategy is to divide and conquer. How many times have you, as a buyer, negotiated with an engineer on your team and had that person hurt you because the engineer's objective was different from yours? This happens frequently. How many times have you, as a seller, negotiated with a factory representative on your team and had that person reduce your effectiveness? How many times have you, as a human resource employee, been hurt by a member of management, manufacturing, and so forth? The point is that if two or more people make up a negotiating team, they *must* have only one set of objectives and one plan (this will be covered in much greater detail later in this book).

*Aims at agreement.* This implies that every negotiation does not have to end in agreement. Many times it is better to walk away from the table than to make a deal. There are thousands of "war stories" concerning the negative impact of bad deals, of orders we should not have won, and so forth.

*Adversary relationship.* This implies that in almost every negotiation the objectives of the opposing sides are very different. (If the objectives were the same, negotiations would not be necessary.) For example, sellers want to get an order at the highest possible price with adequate lead time and in economical production quantities. Buyers on the other side of the table want low price, immediate delivery, and small quantities. In most of our negotiations we will be agents negotiating for our principal. Our opponent is generally in the same position. We must never forget that we owe 100 percent loyalty to our principal and the principal's objectives. This point does *not* mean that the relationship must be filled with conflict, argument, verbal fighting, and so forth. We can have a very fine relationship with our opponent (i.e., a cooperative process), but we must always remember that the person is our opponent.

*Need each other.* We negotiate to develop relationships with others. Buyers need good suppliers to buy from. Sellers need good customers to sell to. Human resource people need labor to work for their company. Labor needs jobs. In most negotiations, both sides need each other. The negotiation process just establishes the rules, regulations, factors, and so forth of the relationship.

*Conducted by agents.* Most of the time we negotiate we are the agent for our principal. When a person buys a car, that person is the agent and principal, but usually the salesperson is just an agent. When a person buys or sells a house, the real estate agent usually performs the largest portion of the negotiations. In business it is very rare that the owner does the actual negotiation. It is essential that you do not forget this point. Your opponent is representing his or her principal and your opponent's behavior may be based upon the principal's demands. This is a significant point. Too many people get emotionally involved in the process. They believe that the "attacks" are personal ones. This is not true. Negotiation is usually an impersonal process between agents representing others.

*Start of a longer relationship.* In sports, when the contest is over, it is over. Nothing can be done to change the score. In May 1983, the Pittsburgh Lacrosse Club's Gold Team defeated the Pittsburgh Lacrosse Club's Black Team by the score of 13 to 11 and the Gold Team won the Allegheny Lacrosse league championship. There is nothing that the Black Team can do about that fact. As long as records are retained, Pittsburgh Lacrosse Club's Gold Team will be the 1983 champion. Of course, Pittsburgh Lacrosse Club's Black Team can say (like the old baseball Brooklyn Dodgers), "Wait till next year," but they must accept the 1983 result. In negotiations the actual negotiation process is just the start of the longer term relationship.

Each side must do what it agreed to do. Buyers, for example, must order what they said they would order, in the quantity they said they would order, on the dates they said they needed it, and pay the agreed upon price, and so forth. Sellers must deliver on the dates, in the quantities, to the specifications, and so forth agreed upon, and the seller must conform to the price and terms of the contract. If they do not, there is much trouble. At the end of a negotiation both sides shake hands with each other. This is really the start, not the end of the relationship.

If your opponent wants to "get even" after the negotiation, he or she will have many opportunities. A seller might ship late, reduce quality, undership, and so forth. A buyer might order significantly less than he or she stated was needed.

During the process, and we will review this point in great detail later, the negotiator must always remember that negotiation is the *start* not the *end*, and the negotiator must govern himself or herself accordingly.

*Psychological process.* Facts do not negotiate. Human beings negotiate. It is possible today to program a buyer's computer so that when a requirement is generated the computer prepares a request for quotation and sends it to all approved suppliers, perhaps by telephone line to the suppliers' computers. The supplier could prepare quotations (or the supplier's computer could prepare it) and send it to the buyer's computer. This computer could be programmed to evaluate the proposals to the .000001 of any and all areas of the purchase decision. The winning supplier would be sent a purchase order (again by telephone line) and the other suppliers would be sent a note saying "better luck next time." Computers can provide tremendous aid to the negotiator, but only aid.

Today, the human element is still most important. Most negotiation is based upon future actions, and many decisions about the future cannot be mechanically predicted. The human ability to consider what will happen in the future, and which of several alternatives is the best, is still a vital element in negotiations. Humans can also evaluate all risk factors.

Since we will negotiate with other humans we must understand the psychology of people, especially in the negotiation process. For example, if a person *believes* that he or she is receiving a good deal (it does not matter whether the deal is good or bad), that person will support it and make it work. If, on the other hand, the person *believes* it is a bad deal (even if the person has won everything, based upon the facts) the person will work against the deal. A professional negotiator works hard at making the opponent believe that he or she has the best of the deal.

*Nonverbal communications.* A good percentage of the communication at the negotiation table is nonverbal. The negotiator must be a good reader of nonverbal communications. Many times a buyer will say "no" or "your price is too high," while the buyer's body is saying "yes." A very good book on this subject is *How to Read a Person Like a Book* by Calero and Nierenberg (Hawthorn Books).

Teachers and seminar leaders must read nonverbal communications. Generally, in any course, the instructor does a lot of talking and the students a lot of listening. Each student nonverbally conveys to the instructor agreement, disagreement, positive reactions, negative reactions, and so forth.

Finally, it should be emphasized that while an adversarial relationship exists in most negotiations, a professional atmosphere must also exist. The statements above concerning negotiation stressed that negotiation is a "cooperative process" that is conducted between "two sides that need each other." A major consideration is that negotiation is the "start of a longer relationship" and is usually conducted by agents.

When a professional atmosphere exists during the negotiation process, it allows those involved to have good relationships before negotiations, during breaks, and after negotiations are completed. Strong business relationships can develop between people who have negotiated with each other over a period of time. A professional atmosphere is a must if the principles we represent are to be successful.

Mutual respect is also a must. This will help the negotiators to find a win-win agreement whenever the situation allows.

There are significant differences between amateur and professional negotiators. One major difference is the atmosphere. A professional atmosphere is a must.

In summary, there are two important points to remember. The first is that the purpose of this book is to help you make a significant impact on your organization. The second is the seven statements describing negotiation, to help you better understand negotiation. Now we can proceed to considering the planning of a negotiation.

# CHAPTER 3

# Planning: The Key to Success

This book covers the most important phase of the negotiation process—planning. One of the truisms of negotiations is that the side that plans the best generally wins the negotiation. There is no excuse for not doing a proper planning job. It has been said that at least 90 percent of success in negotiations is due to thorough preparation. It helps to be able to bluff, to be able to read the other person, and to be well poised at all times. The fact remains that if one adversary in a negotiation has distinctly more knowledge and is much better prepared than the other, it is likely the former will get the best of the bargain.

Planning is the key to winning in every field of endeavor. Vince Lombardi, the great football coach of the Green Bay Packers' dynasty of the 1960s was quoted many times as saying that preparation was 90 percent of winning a football game.

In doing the research for this book, I looked for a business in which luck was more important than planning. Auto racing was the one area that many people suggested. So I took a look at auto racing. This certainly had to be a business in which luck was more important than any other factor in the success of a team. A. J. Foyt, four-time winner of the Indy 500 and a winner of almost every other major auto race in the United States and of the 24 hours of LaMans, said success in racing is when "luck meets preparation." The Wood brothers are a very famous stock car racing team. Glen Wood was quoted as saying, "The problem with most of the teams that run back in the pack is not lack of cubic money, it is mainly a lack of preparation." The point of these two quotes is that in racing luck has a lot to do with success. A car in front of you may blow a tire, you hit that car, and are out of the race. You can do nothing about that. However, the team that is best prepared will have its car last longer (without an accident) than any other car. That car has a better chance of winning. Stock car racing started a long time ago on small dirt tracks in the South. Every team started even, or almost even. The successful teams today are the ones that were best prepared over the years. Each time a race started, their cars were ready. Certainly more ready than the other cars. That is why they are much more successful today.

Another viewpoint comes from Don Cox who joined the Roger Penske team from the General Motors Institute. Mr. Cox stated:

> You've got to be organized. You know what has to be done, who's going to handle what, when to make pit stops. We set up our race strategy beforehand and stick to it. Each driver is different, each car gets a different set-up. There's no room for confusion. If we go organized and prepared and lose the race, that's all right. But, if we're not prepared and we lose, it's inexcusable.

The last part of that statement is also true for negotiations. Cox meant that if our cars and drivers are absolutely ready for the race that is all we can do. If racing luck is against us today, we will lose. But if we are more prepared for every race than our competitors, we will win more races than our competitors. This is also true for negotiations. If you are always more prepared than your opponents, you will win more negotiations. Just as in racing, sometimes in negotiations your opponent will do something that you cannot stop.

The important point is to be more prepared, every time, than your opponent.

I believe that the last part of Cox's statement can be slightly modified to apply to negotiation: "In negotiations, if you go organized and prepared and lose the negotiation, that's okay. But if you are not prepared and you lose, that is inexcusable." The purpose of this book is to give you a process that, if it is followed, will assure that you are more prepared than your opponent in any future negotiation.

One of the most important points of negotiation is that the side that comes out on the long end after a negotiation is generally the side that was best prepared. The reverse is also true. If your opponent comes out best at the end of a negotiation it is usually because you stubbed your toes because you were not prepared.

In many endeavors, planning is the key element in success. In no area is this more true than negotiation. During a negotiation you cannot always control your opponent. You can always control how much you plan and how good it is. It is very possible that your opponent will be irrational and absolutely uncontrollable. (Remember a few years ago when a leader of the USSR banged his shoe on the table at the United Nations?) It could happen that your opponent behaves so that no one could control him or her.

But, and this is a big but, you can control how much you plan. No one can stop you from doing a complete planning job. Before a negotiation the only factor controlling how much you plan is you. If your opponent does more planning than you, it is only because your opponent spent more time planning or spent planning time more effectively.

It really doesn't matter what type of negotiation you are involved in—buyer-seller, labor-management, boss-subordinate—planning is the key to success. It is a very powerful feeling to know that you are completely prepared before a negotiation, to feel that you cannot wait for the negotiation to start because you know that you will do very well.

I spent three years in the U.S. Air Force. I went to navigator training school and after graduating I was retained at the base to become a navigation instructor. I flew in the same type of plane three or four times a week for about three years. The pilots at our base flew the same planes (T-29) four to six times per week. I am sure that any pilot or navigator at our base could, from memory, recite their own checklist backward or forward. They could start at any point on the list and go on to every second, third, fourth item, and so forth, and never make a mistake. You would lose most bets if you bet against the pilot or navigator who was a little sleepy that he could not remember the checklist. Each time we took off, however, we read our checklist point by point. We had to be sure that every point on the checklist was complete before we took off. This is also true of all checklists (after level off, before landing, after landing, and so forth), used by pilots and navigators.

Just like an airplane pilot, a negotiator must have a prenegotiation checklist—a list of all those activities that must be accomplished, and at a high level of quality. The following checklist should be completed before your next negotiation.

Checkpoint  1: Time
Checkpoint  2: Issues to be negotiated
Checkpoint  3: Issues to be avoided
Checkpoint  4: Rate negotiation issues
Checkpoint  5: Value issues to be negotiated
Checkpoint  6: Decide whether team or individual negotiation
Checkpoint  7: Determine your authority limits
Checkpoint  8: Collect the facts
Checkpoint  9: Analyze the other side
Checkpoint 10: Analyze your opponent
Checkpoint 11: Cost analysis negotiation
Checkpoint 12: Analyze the other influences
Checkpoint 13: Evaluate your position
Checkpoint 14: Plan your agenda
Checkpoint 15: Write out your questions
Checkpoint 16: Determine initial positions
Checkpoint 17: Establish your objectives
Checkpoint 18: Determine strategies and tactics
Checkpoint 19: Role-play

Checkpoint 20: Revise your plan

Checkpoint 21: Where and when to negotiate

Checkpoint 22: Analyze self

Checkpoint 23: Be prepared

Checkpoint 24: Document results

Checkpoint 25: Prepare to listen

This book will review each checkpoint in detail and will review all the issues to be considered in your future negotiations. Figure 4-2 (MAP, for "Morrison's Advanced Planner") is a spread sheet recommended for use with this checklist. (See Chapter 4.)

The negotiation checklist was developed to cover all types of negotiations. Some checkpoints will not apply to all negotiations. For example, checkpoint 11 (cost analysis negotiation) will only apply to buyer-seller negotiations; checkpoint 7 (determine your authority limits) may not apply to buying a car; and checkpoint 19 (role play) may not apply to buying a house. Those checkpoints that do not apply can easily be dropped for any specific situation. It is better to review too many items and eliminate some, rather to review too few items and forget some. This is a strong foundation of this book—planning is the key to success. Two words "planning" and "preparation" will be used interchangeably throughout the book. There will not be a difference in definition. This book details all the activities that must come before the start of negotiations and both planning and preparation are words that cover those activities.

Throughout the book examples taken from actual negotiations are provided to illustrate key points. For each instance an example is not given for every type of negotiation (If I did the book would be much larger). Examples could easily be given for each type of negotiation for every point made in the book. Examples from every type of negotiation are in various areas of the book, as the book will apply to every type of negotiation.

In sports in general, and in boxing in particular, it is important that the athlete do his or her own "roadwork." No one can run for a boxer. If the boxer does not run, or "cheats" on his running, no one can help him when he gets into trouble during a bout.

Likewise, the negotiator must do his or her own planning, or be the leader of the planning team. It is not possible to pick up all the planning information, read it the night before, and walk into a negotiation the next day and win. The negotiator must know how all the data, facts, figures, and so forth were determined. The negotiator must know which information is the strongest and which is the weakest. Therefore, all negotiators should do their own "roadwork" to avoid trouble in the negotiation.

Planning as the key to winning will continue to be stressed. But what does winning a negotiation mean? In Chapter 2 it was stressed that negotiation is the start of a longer relationship. This is a very important point to remember, and must govern your behavior at all times. The definition of "winning" is maximizing your principal's objectives. That is, obtaining the largest number of your principal's objectives as possible. In simpler terms, getting the most for your boss or principal.

This does not mean a win-lose attitude. This must be repeated! This does not mean a win-lose attitude. All win-lose negotiations will become lose-lose negotiations. It is possible to completely win a negotiation and have your opponent completely lose a negotiation. But what will happen during the life of the contract or relationship? The loser will "get even." So all win-lose negotiations eventually will become lose-lose negotiations.

The professional negotiator will *always* look for a *win-win* situation. If the situation can be a joint win, that is best of all. Many experts and practitioners preach that successful negotiations are a joint win for both sides. During all negotiations we must look for win-win situations.

If a win-win result is not possible, then the only acceptable situation is: I win—you-think-you-won. It is important to remember that the definition of winning is maximizing your objectives. If your opponent is trying to "get even" then your objectives cannot be maximized. The best way to maximize your objectives is to have your opponent work hard to complete all the conditions of the agreement. Your opponent will only work hard to complete the agreement if he or she believes it is in his or her best interest. So a win-win, or I win—you-think-you-won result must be the objective of all negotiations.

To achieve our objectives, a complete planning job is a must. This book will present all the tools necessary to do a complete planning job. Three areas will be stressed: (1) a 25-point checklist; (2) a planning spread sheet, and (3) consideration of all the issues to be negotiated.

As you plan for each future negotiation, these tools will assure a complete planning job. The size of the negotiation will determine the amount of planning required. The planning process should never be changed.

In Chapter 4 each of the 25 checkpoints is discussed in detail. Each must be completed before any negotiation. Also in Chapter 4 the planning spread sheet is introduced and explained.

# Negotiation Checkpoints

This chapter reviews in detail the 25 checkpoints that must be completed before you negotiate. The checkpoints should be completed in the order listed, as they are designed to build upon each other. The information developed in each checkpoint should be written down and maintained in the negotiation file. Two advantages will happen. First nothing will be forgotten and second you will start building a very complete history file.

## CHECKPOINT 1: TIME

This aspect of time will apply differently to each negotiator depending upon the negotiator's position—buyer, seller, labor representative, management representative, and so forth. It is one of only two checkpoints that will not apply to every buy-sell negotiation in the same way. (The other is Checkpoint 11.)

## The Buyer's Viewpoint

After first considering the needs of your company and then the market conditions, you must decide whether the time is right to negotiate. Two important points must be considered. First, for items you are buying on a repetitive basis you must decide the length of time for your new contracts. A buyer can save two to five percent if he or she buys on the down-side of the business cycle (See Figure 4-1.) A buyer who places a long-term contract at points A, E, H will pay considerably more than a buyer who places a long-term contract at points C and G. Ideally, a buyer wants to place a contract at point C in the business cycle and have it run until point G. The buyer will be going into the market for a new long-term contract at point F in the business cycle. At that time, the short-term future will look very dark and all the suppliers will be very "hungry."

The buyer can negotiate from a point of strength and obtain the very best possible deal. Even using the best forecasting service and all available economic experts, it is impossible to exactly hit the bottom of each business cycle. It is suggested that a proper planning job will allow a buyer to buy at the bottom 10 percent of the cycle. If so,

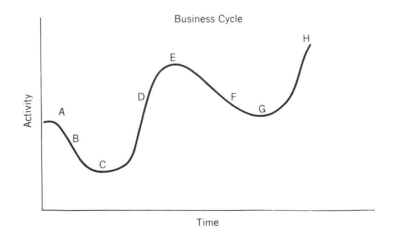

**FIGURE 4-1**   Business cycle

he or she will save two to five percent as compared with a buyer who buys at the top 10 percent of the cycle.

Secondly, a buyer may have several major items to negotiate in the next several months. Since they cannot all be negotiated at once, the buyer should consider the best order to negotiate. At the same moment in time, different businesses can be at different points of the business cycle. As a buyer, the ideal position to start negotiations is point B. The worst is point D. (A, E, and H are not far behind point D.) The sales team across the negotiation table from a buyer when the business cycle is at point B will be in a weak position. The future looks bleak, sales forecasts show a declining market, profit margins are declining at a rapid rate, and there is a lot of pressure to get all the business possible. Winning the order can be much more important to the sales team than winning the negotiation. At point D the sales team is under significantly less pressure and may be in the position of "picking" the orders they want. They want to win the negotiation, not the order.

The buyer's decision of which order to negotiate may be more important than any other single factor in determining the outcome of negotiations. Buyers must give careful consideration to negotiating at the right time.

## The Seller's Viewpoint

In a majority of the buy-sell negotiations the time of the negotiation is determined by the buyer. It is unusual for a seller to contact a buyer and say, "I'm ready to negotiate your next purchase." However, the sales side must attempt to determine why the buyer has decided to negotiate at this time. A careful analysis of all the factors behind the decision will allow the sales team to plot a strategy designed for maximum return.

The ideal situation, for the sales team, is when there is significant pressure on the buyer for delivery. If the buyer needs the item and must have it immediately, the sales team is in a position of strength. It is possible that at point D in the business cycle a buyer may have an urgent need to purchase a certain item. In this case the sales team, if it has done a proper job, has the opportunity to control the negotiations. Thus, whenever a buyer contacts one of his or her suppliers to arrange a future negotiation, the sales team must ask, "Why did the buyer pick this time to negotiate?"

Another important point to consider from the sales side is that a request for quotation (RFQ) is usually the first step in the negotiating process. The sales team must decide how to quote and must allow itself room if the buyer wants to negotiate. The seller must make an important decision concerning the buyer. The buyer has many possible tactics. First, the buyer may review all bids and accept the lowest bid that meets the specificiations. Second, the buyer may negotiate with the lowest three bidders, so the other bidders have no opportunity to get the order. Third, the buyer may negotiate with all responsive bids. In general, it is the buyer's choice. The buyer also has several intermediate options.

The seller must determine, before quoting, which tactic the buyer is using for this purchase. If the seller is wrong, the seller can be in big trouble. For example, if the seller believes the buyer will not negotiate and quotes the seller's lowest possible price and the buyer starts negotiations, the seller, to get the order, may very well lose profit since the buyer will expect some movement. On the other hand, if the seller expects negotiations and quotes high (to allow room to move) and the buyer accepts the lowest quote, the seller will lose the order.

Another point for the seller to consider is a reopener clause. If the buyer has picked point B as the time to negotiate so that the seller is at a disadvantage and the length of the contract to go to point G, another major disadvantage, the seller should work hard to have a clause to reopen the contract at point D or point E. At that time the seller's powerful position should enable him or her to improve the contract terms. The seller may even ask for an extension of time to point H.

## Labor Relations' Viewpoint

The time of a labor negotiation is determined by the contract. Neither side can control this aspect of the negotiation. The key item is the date of the next negotiation, so you must determine when it will be to your advantage to negotiate again. Many factors should be considered.

1.  What is the busiest time of the year for the company?
2.  When will the company's competitor's labor contracts expire?
3.  When will the company's suppliers' labor contracts expire?
4.  When will the company's customers' labor contracts expire?
5.  When will the rate of inflation be the highest in the short-term future?
6.  When is the weather the best? (It is unpleasant to picket in sub-zero weather.)
7.  When is the best time of the year for getting part-time jobs?
8.  When is the best time of the year from a recreation viewpoint? (E.g., the first day of hunting season?)
9.  How fast will the government get involved, if there is a strike?
10. Where will this industry be on the business cycle in the short-term future?

The length of the contract will have a major impact on the results of the next negotiation. It might be better to give a little more now on other issues in order to get the best contract length for your side.

Another example of using time advantageously is labor's submitting a large number of grievances just before the contract expires. This gives them more issues to negotiate (and maybe more to give on) during the actual negotiation.

## CHECKPOINT 2: ISSUES TO BE NEGOTIATED

One of the key differences between the amateur and professional negotiator is that the professional negotiates many issues. The amateur concentrates on only a few.

At the seminars I have conducted for buyers, sellers, or both, the attendees are asked to write on a piece of paper the number of issues they believe should be considered before any buy-sell negotiation. What do you think their answers are? Before reading further take a few minutes to jot down all those you can think of. If your major interest is labor-management, consider your issues. For buyer-seller negotiations a very common answer is one price. These students state that everything else really does not matter. If the price is right, the deal is made. As we will discuss later in this book, price is only one of many issues. All professional negotiators love to negotiate with a person who thinks that price is it. Most of the time it is possible to give on the price issue, get on all of the rest of the issues, and win the overall negotiation.

In general, it is easy to win any one issue in a negotiation (such as lowest price, or on-time delivery), but the attainment of multiple, often conflicting objectives is difficult. Most items conflict, for example, lower price versus higher quality, or tooling cost versus set-up time, or higher productivity versus small wage increase.

In Chapter 5 more than 250 issues that must be considered in a buyer-seller negotiation are listed. This list is very generic. For your specific business you should be able to add 50–100 more issues applicable to your particular situation. For each item being negotiated you must add the technical specifications for that item. For example, a steel buyer must add technical items such as size, thickness, chemistry, grain size, coil size, camber, hardness, and so forth. The buyer-seller negotiation issues list was first developed in 1972. At that time it consisted of 27 issues. Each year many issues have been added. Many of these have been provided by students in my courses. At one time it was felt that the maximum number was "about 100"; now I'm convinced that there is no maximum number.

Chapter 6 reviews more than 200 issues that must be considered in a labor-management negotiation. Again, this list is very generic. Each contract has its own unique areas. Chapter 7 reviews 240 business-business issues to be negotiated. Chapter 8 reviews more than 50 issues to be negotiated when setting up a business meeting. Chapter 9 reviews issues in personal negotiations (House and Car).

These lists should be considered as basic lists only. For each negotiation situation many issues must be added. The more issues you consider, the better your chance of winning.

Figure 4-2 is a blank planning spread sheet that you are strongly encouraged to use for each negotiation. It will be your MAP (Morrison's Advanced Planner) toward better planning and more successful negotiations. As each new concept is introduced, the appropriate column will be filled in to illustrate the concept.

One of the ironies of the business environment is that many people

**FIGURE 4-2** MAP

plan their vacation better than they plan their negotiations. I know many people who start planning a year in advance. They get maps and books to read about the area to be visited. They confirm motel/ hotel reservations (with paid deposits), airline reservations, rent-a-car reservations, and so forth long before they leave. When they return to work they may negotiate a major contract without proper planning. I believe that the better you plan your negotiations, the better the vacation you will be able to afford because you will be more successful on your job.

The procedure for Checkpoint 2 is to review your specific list of issues to be negotiated. Ask yourself these questions:

1.  Is this issue important to this negotiation?
2.  Should I bring this issue up in the negotiation?
3.  Will someone else bring up this issue?

If the answer to any of these questions is yes, write that point in Column 1 (Figure 4-3) on your planning spread sheet (MAP). If the answer is no, just go on to the next point. It should not take too long to complete this checkpoint, but you should completely review the list. Note that the MAP illustrated only has room for four issues. This is just an illustration, and space determined the number of lines. In real world use the MAP will have many lines.

Many times in a negotiation your opponent will bring up an issue that you are not prepared to discuss. Since your opponent is ready and you are not, he or she will probably win the issue. It is most important to have every possible issue to be negotiated on your spread sheet.

Another consideration is that you cannot hide big issues in a negotiation. The big issues will be discussed sometime. They may not be put on the table until very late in the negotiation, but sooner or later they will be on the table. The professional knows this and plans for this. For example, a sales team whose company has been having quality problems must know that sooner or later the buyer will discuss this issue, so they prepare for it. Remember, just as it is impossible to hide a fox in a hen house (without the hens knowing), it is impossible to hide big issues in a negotiation.

**FIGURE 4-3** MAP

31

Checkpoint 2 is a simple procedure. Review your list of all the issues to be negotiated in your business and write down on your MAP form every issue that you believe will be discussed in the specific negotiation that you are planning.

## CHECKPOINT 3: ISSUES TO BE AVOIDED

Many negotiations have been lost by one party, rather than won by the other party. In the world of sports, when a new coach takes over a team that has been losing for several years one of his or her first objectives is to help the team learn how "not to lose."

When we look at the negotiation process we see that in many cases a team loses a negotiation because it negotiated an issue that it was sure to lose. Had that issue not been put on the table, the team might *have had a better chance of winning.* In bridge, for example, the pair that makes the fewest mistakes usually wins most of the bridge tournaments. Once in a while a few brilliant plays will win, but in the long run the steady team that makes the fewest mistakes will win most of the time.

The World Cup is another excellent example. During the 1982 World Soccer Championship Tournament, the president of the Spanish Football Federation was quoted as saying, "A good team is like an accordion, defense most of the time, but able to surge forward for a goal." In other words, make sure you do not make a mistake and let the other team score. Then when you get the opportunity to score, go for it.

In the case studies in seminars I have seen teams raise issues on which they were very weak. In the real world, many accomplished negotiators tell of countless cases where a team initiated the discussion of an issue they were sure to lose. The professional negotiator knows that many of his or her weak points will be discussed by the opponent. He or she also knows that the opponent is human and may make a mistake. The opponent may overlook an issue. The opponent may make a faulty assumption. In short, the opponent may goof. So the professional negotiator knows that he or she should never start the discussion of any issue on which his or her position is weak. This checkpoint, issues to be avoided, requires that the negotiator completely review the list of issues to be negotiated a second time and ask, "Should I avoid any of these issues?" All issues to be avoided should be listed in column 1 of the MAP, below the issues to be negotiated. (See Figure 4-4.) Again note only one line is included in the illustration because of space limitations.

A few examples will demonstrate the importance of this checkpoint. From the buyer's viewpoint an example of an issue to avoid could be cash terms. Many companies today are taking much longer to pay their bills. The price of money today is so high that a few extra days per bill can make a lot of difference at the end of the year in reduced interest costs. If this is the case, the buyer might be wise *not* to ask for better terms. If the supplier's terms have been one percent-10 days and the buyer's company has been taking the one percent, but paying in 20 days, the buyer is in a very poor position to ask for two percent-10 days or one percent-20 days. Once the subject of terms is put on the table the seller might well ask for interest payments after 10 days. In this case the buyer is much smarter if he or she never brings up the subject of terms.

From the seller's viewpoint an example of an issue to avoid could be lead times. If the seller's company has been late recently, the seller had better not talk about faster delivery, or shorter lead times.

In your negotiation areas there are many issues to be avoided. List them in column 1 of the planning spread sheet.

This checkpoint is especially important if a team is to conduct the negotiation. There are thousands of horror stories about a lead negotiator being "shot down" by one of his or her teammates. Teammates want to be part of the negotiation so they open their mouth and say the wrong thing or discuss the wrong point. Most people are very uncomfortable with silence. Your teammate may want to fill "a void" and when doing so may very well discuss a point you will lose. This is especially true of sellers (buy-sell negotiation) and management (labor-management negotiation).

This checkpoint is very important during the planning stage of a team negotiation. At that time everyone on the team agrees that no one will discuss the issues to be avoided.

Note that you must complete all the planning for these issues because your opponent might just bring them up and, if your position is weak to begin with, you want to be as prepared as possible.

| 1 | 2 | 3 | 4 | 5 | 6 | 7 | 8 | 9 | 10 | 11 | 12 | 13 | 14 | 15 | 16 |
|---|---|---|---|---|---|---|---|---|---|---|---|---|---|---|---|
| Issues | | | | | | | | | | | | | | | |
| Cash Terms | | | | | | | | | | | | | | | |
| | | | | | | | | | | | | | | | |
| | | | | | | | | | | | | | | | |
| | | | | | | | | | | | | | | | |
| Avoid Issues | | | | | | | | | | | | | | | |
| Lead Time | | | | | | | | | | | | | | | |

FIGURE 4-4 MAP

## CHECKPOINT 4: RATE NEGOTIATION ISSUES

Each issue to be negotiated must be rated as a must point, a want point, or a give point, defined as follows.

Must Point. An issue that your side must win. An issue without which you will not sign a contract or reach an agreement. An issue that, if you don't get what you want or need, you will walk away from the negotiation table.

Want Point. An issues that is very, very desirable for your side. An issue that you will go to great lengths to win.

Give Point. All other issues.

In column 2 of the planning spread sheet you must put an M, W, or G next to each issue to be negotiated (see Figure 4-5). This identifies the type of issue it is and how you will treat it during negotiation.

Many issues will have three or more levels. An issue may have a give level, a want level, and a must level. An example from the buyer's side might be packing. They buyer may open the negotiation with a position that he or she wants each item individually wrapped (for example, aluminum castings). Each casting must be wrapped with bubble pack. This is his or her give level. A second position (want level) might be that the buyer wants a cell-set type packing. This procedure insures that each casting is in its own separate corrugated cell. Later in the negotiation process the buyer might agree to shell cartons with no inner packing (with seller assuming any damage claims) as his or her must level.

Another example, from the seller's side, could be quantity. The seller will usually ask for 100 percent (or very close to it) of the business to start the negotiation. In many cases this is just a give position. Later the seller may ask for 80 percent (want level) and finally shoot for being the number-one source (51 percent plus) as the must level.

I have found that another way in which amateurs and professional negotiators differ is that amateurs allow themselves little room to move. The professional plans the maximum flexibility possible. During checkpoint 4 be sure to ask yourself, "Can I add intermediate lev-

| | ① | ② | ③ | ④ | ⑤ | ⑥ | ⑦ | ⑧ | ⑨ | ⑩ | ⑪ | ⑫ | ⑬ | ⑭ | ⑮ | ⑯ |
|---|---|---|---|---|---|---|---|---|---|---|---|---|---|---|---|---|
| Issues | | Type | | | | | | | | | | | | | | |
| Cash Terms | | W | | | | | | | | | | | | | | |
| | | | | | | | | | | | | | | | | |
| | | | | | | | | | | | | | | | | |
| | | | | | | | | | | | | | | | | |
| Avoid Issues | | | | | | | | | | | | | | | | |
| Lead Time | | — | | | | | | | | | | | | | | |

**FIGURE 4-5**  MAP

els (between must and want and between want and give) to increase my flexibility?"

If you do not have a lot of give issues, you must add issues to your list of issues to be negotiated. Go back over your master list of all issues to be negotiated (Chapters 5–9) and pick issues that you passed over the first time. Add them to your list in column 1 of the MAP and if necessary, make up some give issues. This will allow you more room to move during the actual negotiation.

In U.S. culture (as in many other cultures), the first offer is very seldom accepted. If you were to visit my home and say, "I'll buy this home for *X* dollars" and the offer was immediately accepted, the very first thing to pop into your mind would be "I paid too much."

Every professional negotiator knows that his or her opponent will originally ask for more than he or she is willing to settle for (points A and C on the negotiation diagram). If a negotiator opens with the position that he or she must sign an agreement then, it is not a negotiation. In reality it is a take it or leave it position. I have watched many case studies in which one side opened with a position very close to its objectives. During the role play that team could not give a point in return for one received and the process broke down. It cannot be stressed too strongly that you must have maximum flexibility as you approach each negotiation.

Flexibility in negotiations is defined as "having an open mind to every offer and every suggestion, and being ready and able to change positions if necessary in order to reach a successful agreement." Negotiators must remember that the objective is to reach a successful agreement for their side (their principals). The negotiator's objective is not to win *his or her way,* but to win.

Many people use the tactic called the "big pot." This means that they ask for a lot of items to start the negotiation. They make the opponent work hard at trying to determine what the want issues, must issues, and give issues. This is especially effective for labor negotiators. The labor side can ask for 60 issues. If management gives labor one of labor's give issues, then labor is ahead. If labor does not get all of its must issues, then the labor side can call a strike.

This checkpoint then requires that during the planning process you rate each issue as a must point, a want point, or a give point. Remember that some issues might have three or more levels. Also remember that it is essential that you have many give issues.

Finally, designate one give issue as your sweetener. This is a give issue to save until the very end of the negotiation, when you are very close to settlement. When your opponent is at the edge of agreement, then you put your sweetener on the table and ask, "If I give you X, can we reach an agreement?" New car salespeople often use this tactic. Most of us have heard a car salesperson say, "If you sign today I'll give you, at no extra charge, an AM-FM 8-track radio, instead of just an AM radio." Many new car salespeople size the buyer up as the buyer enters the showroom and ask themselves, "What sweetener will appeal to this potential buyer?"

The sweetener concept is just as applicable in other types of negotiations. For example, an industrial buyer may hold back some volume. The buyer may negotiate a package for 80,000 items, then ask, late in the negotiation process, "If I order 100,000 items do we have a deal at X price?" The seller now has a 25 percent increase in sales to consider. The seller in an industrial negotiation may save the cost of freight as the sweetener. Late in the negotiation the seller will say, "If we agree to pay the freight will you give us the order today?"

This concept is most important and you should plan at least one (more would be better) sweetener for each negotiation.

Most negotiations are based upon the give and take principle. In our culture this is very true, and most find that it is give-get, not get-give. The professional negotiator understands that it is best to give and then take. In general, it is very hard to convince your opponent to give first. Why should your opponent give first? To be successful you should be prepared to give first (and then of course get). If, during the planning stage of negotiations, you develop many give issues you will be in a superior position during the negotiation. You will be able to give an issue (one that does not hurt your side) and then get an issue that you want.

Another important concept is that you do not win or lose a negotiation in one moment or in a very short time. The process is give and take. To be successful you should have as many give issues as possible. The procedure that most professionals use is to give early and get late.

Checkpoint 4 is a process during which you should rate every issue to be negotiated as a must, want, give, or a combination of these.

## CHECKPOINT 5: VALUE ISSUES TO BE NEGOTIATED

Would you play poker with someone who proposes the following ground rules? Each player puts $50 into the kitty and receives three equal stacks of red, white, and blue chips. At the end of three hours the dealer pays off based on the number of chips each person has in front of him or her at that time. Would you play poker with this person? What are the values of the red chips, the white chips, and the blue chips, you ask. The dealer will tell you as he or she is paying off at the end of the game.

If you do not value the points to be negotiated, you would be negotiating in the same manner as playing poker without knowing the value of the chips. No one would ever start a poker game without knowing the value of each different color of chip. No one should ever start a negotiation without knowing the value of each issue to be negotiated. The value must be determined from two views—yours and your opponent's.

Please refer to the planning spread sheet (MAP) and columns 3 and 6 (Figure 4-6). In column 3 you should record the value of each issue to your side. (Vm stands for Value-me.) In column 6 you should record the value of each issue to your opponent's side. (Vo stands for Value-opponent.)

The values in both of these columns should be shown in dollars. Business is run in dollars and cents and the value of the issues to be negotiated must be in dollars and cents. The tolerance on Vm should be zero. The tolerance on Vo will be ± three percent or better based upon how much you know about your opponent. Many feel this is difficult, that many issues cannot be reduced to an objective value. However, almost every conceivable issue can be listed this way. In buyer-seller negotiations, for example, consider lead time. To value this, determine the value of one week's usage of the item being negotiated and multiply by the cost of carrying your inventory. Each week's reduction in lead time will result in a savings of this value. An-

| Issues | 1 | 2 | 3 | 4 | 5 | 6 | 7 | 8 | 9 | 10 | 11 | 12 | 13 | 14 | 15 | 16 |
|---|---|---|---|---|---|---|---|---|---|---|---|---|---|---|---|---|
| | | Type | $V_M$ | | | $V_O$ | | | | | | | | | | |
| Cash Terms | | W | 1% = $2,700 | | | 1% = $2,700 | | | | | | | | | | |
| | | | | | | | | | | | | | | | | |
| | | | | | | | | | | | | | | | | |
| | | | | | | | | | | | | | | | | |
| Avoid Issues | | — | $5,000/ week | | | $10,000/ week | | | | | | | | | | |
| Lead Time | | | | | | | | | | | | | | | | |

**FIGURE 4-6** MAP

40

other example is quality. To value this, determine the total cost of each rejection (inspection time, transportation, material handlers, lost production, etc.). Determine the rejection percentage and apply it to the total value of the items being negotiated.

Nearly everything in business can be reduced to some objective value system. If you wanted to measure the morale of a manufacturing plant, it would be very easy. Most people would state that it is impossible to objectively rate morale, but this is not true. Here are just a few ways to use to get an accurate measurement:

1. Turnover rate
2. Absentee rate
3. Number of late slips
4. Number of employee-caused rejections
5. Number of relatives who apply for work
6. Cleanliness of plant
7. Productivity rate
8. Rejection rate
9. Number of grievances

There are many more. The point is that in business we want objective indicators of performance and in negotiations we want to have the value for each issue to be negotiated in objective terms (i.e., dollars and cents).

Another way to remember this is by the lesson I learned from my first boss. The boss said, "You give me intangible results and I will give you intangible pay." It is very hard to buy a week's groceries with intangible pay. The boss added, "If you expect to receive dollars from the company then the company can expect dollars from you." The same is true for negotiations. The company expects dollar results from its negotiators. During the planning stage of a negotiation you must determine the dollar value of each issue to be negotiated.

The importance of this checkpoint cannot be stressed strongly enough. So many times during the negotiating process you will hear, "I'll give you this issue, if you give me that issue." If you do not know the values of "this" and "that" issue to both you and your opponent, how can you agree or disagree? Do you have a good deal or a bad deal? Is it a good trade or a bad trade? If your opponent has done his or her homework on this checkpoint and you have not, your opponent will take you to the cleaners, trading low value issues for high value issues.

No one wins a negotiation with one trade of issues. The professional wins a little with each trade, giving up three to get seven, five to get eight, 11 to get 13, 27 to get 35, and so forth. At the end of the negotiation the professional has much more value on his or her side of the table.

Thousands of times in the case studies conducted in my seminars, I have seen one side give away an issue without ever considering its value. Buyers often agree to pay the freight for a small price concession. In today's environment a price reduction is good, but the net value of the trade to the buyer is a negative one. If buyers do not know the value in dollars of the transportation cost, they may feel that it is better to get a "sure thing" with a price reduction. This is very bad in a case study; it is a catastrophe in the real world.

Students ask how close can we get to the real value when we are in the planning process. I know that the deviation for $V_m$ should be $\pm$ 0. You can get the exact values for your side. No question about it. I strongly believe that the deviation for $V_o$ should be $\pm$ three percent. If you know anything about the item being negotiated, you should be able to get very, very close to your opponent's exact numbers. As the actual negotiation progresses, you may be able to zero in on the opponent's values.

Finally, there is another important concept concerning the value of the issues to be negotiated. During the actual negotiation as you give and get issues, the value of the remaining issues may very well change. For example, if you win a very important, high value, must point, the value of some of your smaller issues may decrease. On the other hand, if you lose a high value issue or two, the value of the remaining issues will increase significantly. Columns 4 and 5 (Figure 4-7) are to be used during the negotiation for revised values. ($V_{mr}$ stands for value-to-me-revised.) ($V_{or}$ stands for value-to-opponent-revised.) Again these should be in money terms. It is important to remember columns 4 and 5 during the negotiation and fill them in.

In summary this checkpoint is the second most important of all.

| 1 | 2 | 3 | 4 | 5 | 6 | 7 | 8 | 9 | 10 | 11 | 12 | 13 | 14 | 15 | 16 |
|---|---|---|---|---|---|---|---|---|----|----|----|----|----|----|----|
| Issues | Type | $V_M$ | $V_{MR}$ | $V_{OR}$ | $V_O$ | | | | | | | | | | |
| Cash Terms | W | 1% = $2,700 | | | 1% = $2,700 | | | | | | | | | | |
| Avoid Issues | | | | | | | | | | | | | | | |
| Lead Time | — | $5,000/ week | | | $10,000/ week | | | | | | | | | | |

**FIGURE 4-7** MAP

You have no alternative but to determine the value of each issue to be negotiated, as well as each issue to be avoided in case your opponent discusses those. During the planning process you must fill in completely, in dollars, Columns 3 (Vm) and 6 (Vo).

## CHECKPOINT 6: DECIDE WHETHER TEAM OR INDIVIDUAL NEGOTIATES

At this stage in the planning process the decision must be made whether the negotiation will be conducted by a team or by one individual. There are advantages to both methods.

### Team Negotiation

The team approach provides more brainpower. It allows for many viewpoints, thus increasing the probability of success. A team negotiation allows the use of experts. There are several considerations in picking a team. First, only have outstanding negotiators on your team. Many times we have a person on our team because "it is his project," or because "the person is the expert on the subject," or because "the person is the boss." This is absolutely wrong. You should only allow people who know how to negotiate to be on the team. Chuck Noll, the most successful coach of the four-time (as of 1985) world champion Pittsburgh Steelers, is famous for his approach to drafting the best athlete available. When you are setting up your negotiating team you must draft the best negotiator available. It is much better to keep people off the team and risk hurting their feelings than it is to let them be on the team and lose the negotiation. If you must include a particular person on your team, at least send him or her to a negotiation training course. Help the person to improve negotiating skills. A technical person can be a tremendous help as a resource person during a negotiation. Remember when selecting team members that they are there not to engineer, or draft, or design, but to negotiate.

Wilt Chamberlain was a great athlete, but he does not hold any National Football League records. He was a great basketball player.

It was nothing against him to say he could not play football. By the same token, a person can be a great person and do a fine job but not be a good negotiator.

A second consideration is that the team can have only one leader. In football, the quarterback is the only person who is supposed to talk in the huddle. The quarterback's job is to run the team. He is totally responsible for deciding what play will be run. The other members of the team are responsible for carrying out the play to the best of their abilities. In negotiations it is exactly the same. Only one person can negotiate in any given negotiation. The rest of the team members are there only as resource persons, to be used as the lead negotiator decides is best for the team. Many times in a negotiation the negotiator says something early to set up a point later in the negotiations, that is, preparing his or her position for gains at a later stage. Only one person can do this successfully. If two people are trying to do this at the same time, it can lead to serious problems. It is, however, possible to have different people lead different parts of a negotiation. For example, the quality control manager may be the team leader during the "quality" section, the engineering manager may be the leader during the "technical" section, and the purchasing manager may be the leader during the "commercial" section. This takes a lot of planning and coordinating. However, it is much better if only one person is the leader for the entire negotiation (both planning and actual negotiation).

A third consideration is the time it takes to plan. Many times your resource people cannot spare the time it takes to plan a negotiation. I believe it is best to have the team members submit information, as requested, to the team leader. The leader will do most of the specific planning.

A fourth consideration is the availability of your resources. It is a fact that many times a secretary decides who will be on the negotiations team. For example, a buyer may call the quality control section and ask who is available two weeks from Tuesday to sit down and talk to ABC Company. The secretary looks over the sign-out sheets and says, "I'll schedule person X." Also, it is hard to schedule several people for a negotiation. In today's business environment very few companies have the luxury of extra personnel.

A fifth consideration is that team negotiations tend to be much longer than individual negotiations. It is almost a law that the time to complete a negotiation increases exponentially with the number of people on the team.

## Individual Negotiation

The individual approach has many advantages. One of the most significant is that no one can disrupt your plans. You have complete control of the situation. The individual approach tends to be much faster. However, the most important advantage is that you can be more open as an individual, especially in a one-on-one negotiation. With a lot of people in the room we tend to be more careful about what we say. In a one-on-one negotiation I can tell my opponent things that will never be quoted but can help settle the deal.

## Numbers Tactics

Many times we see that the sides of a negotiation "even up." This is an important concept. The sale's team, for example, may bring the salesperson, the district sales manager, and the application engineer. The buyer will feel compelled to include his or her boss (the purchasing manager), and a materials engineer. In buyer-seller negotiations both sides usually have the same number of people. You will want to consider using this to your advantage. For example, assume you are faced with a buyer who stonewalls you, never allowing you to talk directly to an engineer. The next time you have a negotiation with that company, bring a team with you. This tactic may just allow you to open up a line of communication with the engineer.

Another tactic, frequently seen in labor negotiations, is to outnumber the opposition. This is done to confuse the opposition and gain advantages.

The final decision whether to negotiate with a team or an individual is most important in deciding the eventual outcome of the negotiation. All the potential alternatives should be reviewed before making a decision. My own preference is to negotiate by myself. This way I can control everything. For very technical negotiations, I will bring one engineer or technical person.

## CHECKPOINT 7: DETERMINE YOUR AUTHORITY LIMITS

At this stage of the planning process it is necessary to meet with your principal and determine the limits of your authority for each issue to be negotiated. In column 7 you must list your authority limit (Figure 4-8). This is important for several reasons. First, if you ever make a deal and your principal does not back you up, you are finished as a negotiator. If you are a buyer the word will quickly spread among the salespeople not to waste their time with you. Everyone will steer clear of you. They will only negotiate with your boss, or your boss's boss, someone whom your principal trusts.

Second, if you are hesitant about your authority you will be less successful. A negotiator who knows his or her limits can be very forceful and self-assured. This negotiator can make statements and take positions with the knowledge that he or she will be backed up completely. A wishy-washy negotiator does not gain the respect of his or her opponent.

It is possible that you may have to negotiate greater authority limits with your principal before the negotiation in order to give you greater flexibility during the negotiation. In the upper right hand corner of the MAP is a line on which your principal can sign this form. This is an "official" way for you to get approval for your plan (Figure 4-9).

A most important point is to never admit, during the negotiation, that you have full authority. Never tell your opponent you can make an agreement. If you get into trouble during a negotiation it is always nice to be able to say, "I will have to review this proposal with my boss before a final agreement." This is a great way to get out of trouble. Of course, at any time during a negotiation you can shake hands and confirm an agreement if the proposal is what you want.

If you are asked by your opponent, "Do you have authority to negotiate?" I suggest you reply, "Yes." If the opponent asks, "Can you

| Issues (1) | Type (2) | Vm (3) | Vmr (4) | Vor (5) | Vo (6) | Authority Limit (7) | (8) | (9) | (10) | (11) | (12) | (13) | (14) | (15) | (16) |
|---|---|---|---|---|---|---|---|---|---|---|---|---|---|---|---|
| Cash Terms | W | 1% = $2.700 | | | 1% = $2.700 | Net in 30 days | | | | | | | | | |
| Avoid Issues | | | | | | | | | | | | | | | |
| Lead Time | — | $5.000/ week | | | $10,000/ week | Max 13 weeks | | | | | | | | | |

**FIGURE 4-8** MAP

48

| | (1) | (2) | (3) | (4) | (5) | (6) | (7) | (8) | (9) | (10) | (11) | (12) | (13) | (14) | (15) | (16) |
|---|---|---|---|---|---|---|---|---|---|---|---|---|---|---|---|---|
| | Issues | Type | $V_M$ | $V_{MR}$ | $V_{OR}$ | $V_O$ | Authority Limit | | | | | | | | | |
| Cash Terms | | W | 1% = $2.700 | | | 1% = $2.700 | Net 30 days | | | | | | | | | |
| | | | | | | | | | | | | | | | | |
| | | | | | | | | | | | | | | | | |
| | | | | | | | | | | | | | | | | |
| Avoid Issues | | — | $5,000/ week | | | $10,000/ week | Max 13 weeks | | | | | | | | | |
| Lead Time | | | | | | | | | | | | | | | | |

A. W. Boss
Signature

**FIGURE 4-9** MAP

49

make a deal today?" I suggest you reply, "Yes, if the deal is within the limits imposed upon me by my principal."

## CHECKPOINT 8: COLLECT THE FACTS

This is an ongoing step. Throughout the planning process the negotiator is collecting facts. There are four important aspects to this checkpoint.

### What is a Fact?

There is a tremendous difference between facts on the one hand and opinions, attitudes, prejudices, belief, assumption, and ideas on the other. In a negotiation you may find yourself in trouble if you do not have the correct information. If your opponent proves you wrong on any point or any data you present in the negotiation, he or she will continue to attack your statements throughout the negotiation. Negotiation at times is like a sports event (football, hockey, etc.) in that once one side establishes momentum, it is very hard for the other side to stop the momentum. One easy way to establish momentum is to prove that the other side does not have the correct data or that its "facts" are not really facts.

Much too often in negotiation we let our opinions, attitudes, or ideas replace facts. Attitudes come from our personal experiences, our prejudices, and our beliefs rather than from hard facts. Attitudes are affected by our past association with people. Many of our attitudes are very deeply rooted.

Assumptions are very similar. If you substitute assumptions for facts you could put yourself in a poor negotiating position. A seminar participant once related an experience that proves how dangerous it is to make assumptions in the negotiation process. She was the purchasing manager for a large firm. One day a negotiation was planned with a potential supplier. The morning of the negotiation the purchasing manager was at her secretary's desk getting a file. The desk was near the entrance door. A man approached her and said, "I'm Mr. XXXXXXX from XXXXXX Company" [the potential supplier]. The sales manager was taken to the hospital last night. It was decided that since we want to make the first sale to you, we would not ask for a delay. I'll negotiate today for my company. Where will the negotiation be held?" The purchasing manager said, "Down that hall, third door on the left, for the morning's technical session."

The man said, "Thanks! And by the way, get me a cup of coffee and bring it to the room." The purchasing manager said, "Okay; do you want cream and sugar?" The man said, "Both."

When the purchasing manager took the coffee to the room the man said, "Will there be seven people from your company? If so, I need three more sets of materials. Make them right now." The purchasing manager said "Okay" and she completed the task.

The purchasing manager, of course, knew that the man had assumed that she was a secretary. She also knew that her time would come. In the afternoon she would lead the commercial session of the negotiation.

That afternoon the man was sent to the purchasing manager's office. He knocked on the door, took two steps into the office, and saw the purchasing manager behind the desk working on some papers. After an appropriate time period, she looked up and said, "Get me a cup of coffee before we start our discussions." The man asked, "Do you want cream or sugar?" The purchasing manager said, "Just black."

Who do you think was in the power position of that negotiation? I am sure that everyone can see that the purchasing manager had the upper hand and that she negotiated a very good deal for her company.

This is just one example of how much trouble you can get into by making the wrong assumption in the negotiation process. A book could be written on that subject alone.

Whenever you use any data in the planning of a negotiation you must ask this question for each individual piece of information: *How can I prove this to be true, beyond any possible doubt and under all possible attacks?* For each item of data, you must be absolutely able to prove the item to be true, or you cannot use it as a fact.

## Keep Emotions out of the Way

The purchasing manager in the previous example demonstrated an important characteristic of successful negotiation. All successful negotiators are thinking-feeling individuals, not feeling-thinking.

To be successful you cannot let your feelings and emotions get in the way. Too often a person lets his or her personal feeling effect his or her behavior and the person does something inappropriate as a result. In negotiations this can be very disastrous.

## NOTE LOCATION OF INFORMATION

Column 8 in our MAP (Figure 4-10) should be filled in with the location of the information—a file name or a notebook tab number. This column will help you to organize your material in a logical, rational, objective manner.

## USE AUTHORITY

Whenever you use facts in a negotiation always refer to an authority from whom you got the fact. Also, use numbers that are to the second or third decimal point. The reason for this is illustrated by the following. Which of these two statements is more believable?

1.   While planning for this negotiation I reviewed our quality records. They show that your rejection rate is about 6 percent and we believe it must improve.

2.   Last week while planning this negotiation I had a long meeting with our director of quality control and quality assurance. The director reviewed all the information at the inspection stations and stated that during the last 14 months your rejection rate was 6.127 percent. This must be improved.

Most people would agree that the second statement seems more believable. That is because it referred to an authority (director of quality control and assurance), gave an exact time period (14 months), and a very exact number (6.127 percent). About the only way to get a number to the third decimal point is to divide two *actual* numbers.

Negotiations might be lost if the other side uses an "authority." For

A. M. Boss
Signature

| ① Issues | ② Type | ③ $V_M$ | ④ $V_{MR}$ | ⑤ $V_{OR}$ | ⑥ $V_O$ | ⑦ Authority Limit | ⑧ Information | ⑨ | ⑩ | ⑪ | ⑫ | ⑬ | ⑭ | ⑮ | ⑯ |
|---|---|---|---|---|---|---|---|---|---|---|---|---|---|---|---|
| Cash Terms | W | 1% = $2,700 | | | 1% = $2,700 | Net 30 days | 2 | | | | | | | | |
| | | | | | | | | | | | | | | | |
| | | | | | | | | | | | | | | | |
| | | | | | | | | | | | | | | | |
| Avoid Issues | | | | | | | | | | | | | | | |
| Lead Time | — | $5,000/ week | | | $10,000/ week | Max 13 weeks | 7 | | | | | | | | |

**FIGURE 4-10**  MAP

53

example, consider the purchasing manager who was in the process of negotiations for his die-cast aluminum requirements for the next year. Some of the major problems were the supplier's capacity, which die inserts would fit into which dies, and how long it would take to change over from one drawing item to another. After some time the buyer and the salesperson concluded they did not have enough information. The seller suggested that they call the factory and have the factory send a production person to answer all the questions.

The next day when the production person arrived, the purchasing manager accepted the person as an expert, assuming that he came from production because he fit the stereotype:

1.   He wore a brown worn jacket and blue pants that did not match.
2.   His tie was at least nine years out of style.
3.   He wore safety shoes.
4.   There still was some grease under his fingernails.
5.   His shirt collar was turned up.

Yes, he fit the stereotype. At the start of the negotiation he said, "I don't know anything about negotiation so I'll just sit here. If you need any facts, just ask me." (He sat at the end of the table.) Whenever the seller or the buyer asked him a question he looked in his (dirty) notebook and answered. Not once did the seller or buyer question his answers. He was the expert.

The purchasing manager conceded later that he lost because of his blind acceptance of the "expert." This gives us two ideas to remember in planning a negotiation. First, never accept at face value any expert that the other side uses. Be prepared to question the person in great detail. (See Checkpoint 15.) Second, plan to use as many experts and authorities as possible for your side.

As the planning continues, mark any data about which you must make an assumption with an identifying symbol. This symbol will remind you that you cannot use the information as a fact. In Checkpoint 15 we will discuss how to test assumptions.

## CHECKPOINT 9: ANALYZE THE OTHER SIDE

You should know a lot about the other side. A good place to start is with annual reports. You should collect annual reports of all the companies that you are currently negotiating with and all those you might negotiate with. The basic information contained in annual reports is the foundation for analyzing the other side.

I know of one purchasing manager who buys one share of stock in every current and potential supplier. As a stockholder the purchasing manager receives an annual report every year, proxy information, and other inside information. This is completely legal. Stock is sold on the public market and anyone can buy it. The funds come from his company and all dividend checks go into the employee picnic or Christmas party fund. Also, as soon as he receives the stock certificate he signs it over to his company and gives the certificate to the controller.

The next step is to reveiw the past year's relationship between your company and your opponent's company. Factual data should be developed to prove the following:

1.  Delivery performance index
2.  Number of late deliveries
3.  Percentage of late deliveries
4.  Percentage of units delivered late
5.  Quality performance index
6.  Number of rejected parts
7.  Percentage of units rejected
8.  Number of unacceptable lots
9.  Percentage of unacceptable lots
10. What percent of the market the company holds
11. Recent actual gross sales billed
12. GSB trend
13. Number of innovative ideas presented
14. Number of cost improvement ideas presented

15. Where this product is on the product life cycle curve
16. Where this product is on the learning curve
17. When your and your opponent's next labor contracts expire

Buyers must develop facts to answer the following *very important* questions. First, how important is this order *and the total account to the company?* Second, how important is this order *and the total account to the region and district office?* Third, how important is this order *and the total account to the salesperson?* This is most significant.

Sellers must develop facts to answer these questions. How important is the commodity to the buyer and the buyer's product? Is this an order-by-order item or an inventory control item?

It is also important to look ahead. Develop information in the following areas.

1. What is the market percentage of your opponent's organization?
2. How does the recent past affect the near- and long-term future?
3. Will capacities change in the future?
4. What is the product cost ratio and will it change?
5. Are there any innovations, technical terms, patents, and so forth in development that will affect the product?
6. Will any government actions affect the future?

Finally, the most important data you can develop about your opponent is *what your opponent's objectives are* in this negotiation. In column 12 of the MAP form you should write in what you believe your opponent's objective is for each point to be negotiated. You should also write a summary page of what you think the opponent's overall objectives are in this negotiation. This is essential. (See Figure 4-11.)

Many times the most obvious objective is not the actual objective. Two examples will prove this point. The first illustrates the fact that most of the time a seller believes that the buyer's objective is to cut price and increase value and the seller develops a plan to hold the line. In one plant the primary objective was to train a work force that had little manufacturing experience. The plant manager wanted "all other things equal" so he could determine how his employee training program was progressing. He told the purchasing manager not to

| ① | ② | ③ | ④ | ⑤ | ⑥ | ⑦ | ⑧ | ⑨ | ⑩ | ⑪ | ⑫ | ⑬ | ⑭ | ⑮ | ⑯ |
|---|---|---|---|---|---|---|---|---|---|---|---|---|---|---|---|
| Issues | Type | $V_M$ | $V_{MR}$ | $V_{OR}$ | $V_O$ | Authority Limit | Information | | | | $O_O$ | | | | |
| Cash Terms | W | 1% = $2,700 | | | 1% = $2,700 | Net 30 days | 2 | | | | 1% in 10 days | | | | |
| Avoid Issues / Lead Time | — | $5,000/ week | | | $10,000/ week | Max 13 weeks | 7 | | | | 13 weeks | | | | |

**FIGURE 4-11** MAP

change suppliers. The plant manager wanted all the material to be constant, so that any variation in product quality would be isolated as due to employee problems, not material problems. Also, the plant manager wanted material available at all times in his plant so that the training of new people would never be interrupted. The purchasing manager negotiated with the current suppliers (the ones that he had to buy from) as hard as he could and gave every indication that he had maximum flexibility. The manager even delayed negotiations to give the impression that he was negotiating with other suppliers. Many times, he received significant concessions, especially price concessions. If those sellers had spent time reviewing what the purchasing manager's objectives were in this *specific negotiation,* they would have made more money.

The other example illustrates the importance of the buyer's knowledge about the seller. One of my seminar participants purchased gasoline in very large quantities on an annual contract basis. He sent requests for quotes each year to seven suppliers and divided the business into equal thirds, by volume. This would assure supply if one company had trouble. It was his practice to review the quotes, call each supplier to give them a "tentative appraisal" of the quote. He reserved two days, if any company wanted to review their quote in person, before he placed the business.

What was the objective of the suppliers? Did a company want to have the lowest price to assure that they would get the order? The purchasing manager thought so. But he was wrong. The objective of each supplier quoting to him was to be third lowest. At that level they would get one third of the volume (the maximum possible) and receive the most money for that volume (because their price was the highest per unit).

Once this was pointed out to the purchasing manager he changed his tactics, and made a significant price savings on his next gasoline negotiation. This was only accomplished because the purchasing manager analyzed the objectives of his opponent.

## CHECKPOINT 10: ANALYZE YOUR OPPONENT

During this step you should write one to three pages about the person or persons you will be negotiating with. Remember that each person: (1) is an individual; (2) is usually an agent for a principal; (3) has many attitudes, opinions, prejudices, ideas, and so forth that may be different from yours; (4) could be under other pressures at the time of the negotiations; and (5) has very strong points and very weak points.

It is also important to remember that there will be four sets of needs at the negotiation table: (1) the needs of your company or your principal; (2) your needs; (3) your opponent's needs; and (4) the needs of your opponent's company or your opponent's principal.

Many people do not understand this point. An example will illustrate it. It is December 10th and a salesperson is negotiating with an account for an order that will be over $50,000. This salesperson's company is producing at 97 percent capacity and has extended lead times. This salesperson is $27,000 short of making his sales objective for the year. Reaching the sales objective entitles the salesperson and spouse to a two-week, all-expense-paid vacation trip to Spain.

On December 10th, the salesperson has a very high need to get the order. The person will agree to just about anything (cut price, improve quality, etc.). However, on December 10th, the company's need to get the order is much lower. The company will not have a strong need to go to any length to win the order. Its position may be take it or leave it.

In this example the needs of the salesperson and the company are very different even though they are on the same side of the negotiations table. A negotiations professional will analyze the opponent to try to get the opponent's needs and/or the opponent's company's need to work for him or her.

In analyzing your opponent, you may find it helpful to review the Maslow Triangle of needs, described in *Motivation and Reasonality* by A. Maslow (Harper and Brothers). Maslow states that there are five levels of basic needs (Hierarchy of Needs). Starting from the bottom, they are

1. Survival (physiological) needs (bottom)
2. Security (safety) needs
3. Belonging (love) needs
4. Esteem needs
5. Self-realization needs (top)

In negotiations your opponent has a hierarchy of needs in relation to the current proposal. If you can use this to your advantage you should. For example, if you are on the purchasing side of a negotiation, the salesperson's "hierarchy of needs," if he or she does not get the order, may be

1.  Will get fired
2.  No merit increase
3.  No promotion
4.  My pride will be hurt
5.  My image will be hurt
6.  It's okay
7.  Nothing will happen

The need level that the buyer perceives the salesperson to have will determine the buyer's tactics and strategies. In Checkpoint 18, this will be discussed in greater detail.

You should ask yourself what strategies and tactics you expect your opponent to use during the negotiation. There are hundreds of identified strategies and tactics that have been used in negotiations. If you can anticipate a strategy and be prepared to defeat it, you will improve your success rate in negotiations.

Football is the best example in which both sides do a lot of preparation in defense of the other side's plans. For example, as a football coach, if I know that 90 percent of the time in third down and two yards to go situations, my next opponent will run the fullback over center, I can prepare a defense to stop the fullback. Of course if I adjust too much, a pass may score a touchdown so I cannot go too far. I can, however, increase the probability that the play will be stopped.

The very same idea is true in negotiations. If as a negotiator I can anticipate your "plays" before the negotiation, I can defend against them and stop you short.

In summary, this planning step requires you to analyze the four sets of needs at the negotiation table, the hierarchy of your opponent's needs, and your opponent's strategies and tactics. When you do, three pages of information will be very easy to fill. You may find that your data will take more than three pages. If it does, you will be even better prepared to negotiate.

## CHECKPOINT 11: COST ANALYSIS NEGOTIATION

One style of negotiation is called cost analysis negotiation. This style is a detailed step-by-step analysis of each element of cost of the item being negotiated, to determine whether the price is fully justified by all of the costs. When dealing with many U.S. government departments on large orders, a cost analysis form is required. Long seminars are conducted to teach people how to use this form. That process will not be duplicated here but some discussion of cost analysis negotiation is in order because in negotiations not requiring a form, a cost analysis style can be very effective, from either the buyer's or seller's side. Generally, however, it is more effective when used by the buyer.

### Five Types of Costs

For use in the negotiation process, the costs should be divided into five areas: direct material costs, direct labor costs, indirect factory costs, indirect office costs, and profit.

Many sellers are reluctant to furnish this data. They feel that how they arrive at their selling price is none of the buyer's business. A good point for the buyer to make is that this position closes the door to any ideas that the buyer or the buyer's engineers might come up with to improve the product or reduce manufacturing cost. These ideas could help in any area of the manufacturing process.

Many times a new set of eyes sees the product differently and can make important suggestions. These suggestions could include new methods for designing the product, for purchasing the raw material, for tooling, for set-up reductions, for manufacturing process, for making assemblies, for packing, for shipping, and so forth. In many cases, the ideas suggested will save the supplier money. More importantly, it may save the supplier money on all items manufactured and/ or increase gross sales billed. This technique is one that really makes the negotiation process a creative, analytical, and factual process as compared to simply picking the low bid and/or haggling about prices.

Many companies have separate cost/price analysis groups who work full-time on analyzing the costs of all items purchased. This group may be part of the purchasing department, or it may be completely independent. With this type of support, the negotiator can come to the negotiations table fully prepared. Even if your company doesn't have a cost/price analysis section, you can still use this technique in future negotiations. The first step is to understand the five elements of cost.

1. ***Direct Costs.*** These are costs that vary directly with each unit produced. For example, if you were manufacturing pencils, the eraser would be a direct cost. For each pencil you would require one eraser. There are two types of direct costs.

   a. *Direct Material Costs.* These consist of raw materials, purchased parts, and subcontract items.

   b. *Direct Labor Costs.* These consist of all costs of actual labor that vary directly with production. A punch press operator is a good example of a direct labor cost.

2. ***Indirect Costs.*** These costs are fixed, semi-variable, or totally variable. There is no direct relationship between production and these costs. An example would be depreciation. If you manufacture 100 or 1,000, or 1 million parts, the cost of depreciation is the same.

   a. *Indirect Factory Costs.* All indirect costs generated in the manufacturing areas are included. An example would be maintenance employees, setup people, and material handlers. Their work does not and cannot be tied directly to production.

   b. *Indirect Office Costs.* This is generally called general and administrative costs. These costs include such functions as purchasing, accounting, engineering, traffic, top management, and so forth. Salespeople paid by salary would fall in this category, as would utilities, office supplies, and so forth.

3. ***Profit.*** For the purpose of a cost analysis, profit is considered a cost to the buyer.

From the buyer's viewpoint, cost negotiation involves three steps: (1) seeking information from the supplier; (2) determining the five types of costs; and (3) negotiating them with the seller.

## Seeking Information from Supplier

First, the buyer should ask the supplier to provide information. The buyer should ask the salesperson to identify the types of raw materials he or she buys and the price for each item. The salesperson should also be asked to identify which components are subcontracted to other sources and the actual prices paid, along with all the purchased parts and their prices. The buyer should also request the finished weight of each part as used in the final product. Any other major elements of direct material costs should also be identified.

The buyer should also ask for direct labor costs, including detail concerning the different types of labor required to manufacture the product, fabrication, assembly, and so forth. The buyer should then ask for the exact number of hours needed for each step in the process and the applicable wage rate for each labor grade. By multiplying hours by rates, the supplier will be able to provide direct labor costs.

In general, there is a relationship between direct labor costs and indirect factory costs. The buyer should ask for this ratio or for exact indirect factory costs.

The total of direct material, direct labor, and indirect factory costs is generally called product cost or factory cost. Most companies will apply a percentage to product cost to determine indirect office costs. The buyer again should ask for this percentage or for the exact cost that applies to the buyer's order. For our purpose, adding product cost and indirect office cost determines total cost. A percentage is added to this for profit, in order to determine proposed selling price.

## DETERMINING THE FIVE TYPES OF COSTS

## Determining Direct Material Costs

To determine direct material costs, the buyer needs two pieces of information: (1) how much material and (2) what it costs. To determine how much material there is in a product, the buyer must make out a bill of material (BOM). This is just a simple list of all the parts that make up the final product. The easiest way to accomplish this is to take the product apart, put the pieces on the table, measure and weigh them, and make out the BOM. This is not too difficult with smaller parts, but would be hard for a power plant. For large items such as that, the buyer must refer to detailed drawings. Figure 4-13 is a bill of material for the calendar stand illustrated in Figure 4-12. Each item on the bill of material must include dimensions, weight, and material.

To determine how much these items cost, the buyer uses his or her own knowledge of market prices and/or contacts other members of the purchasing department in the buyer's company. This is one of the easiest parts of doing a cost analysis. The buyer must consider not only market price, but also whether the supplier is obtaining any quantity discounts or can get these items from other divisions in the supplier's company at a reduced cost.

When determining direct material costs, the tolerance of error should be very small. Since how much material is needed is figured by actually taking the item apart, this should be exact ± 0. The prices

**FIGURE 4-12**   Desk calendar

| | | | |
|---|---|---|---|
| 1. | Base | Steel 4 × 6 inches | 1 each |
| 2. | Nameplate | Aluminum 4 × 1 inches | 1 each |
| 3. | Screws | Steel | 2 each |
| 4. | Gromets | Rubber | 2 each |

**FIGURE 4-13**  Bill of material

should be very close. A knowledgeable buyer should be able to figure the exact market prices and should be able to come close on discounts, and so forth. The error here should be no larger than ± one percent.

When determining the direct material costs, the buyer must consider scrap. There are two types of scrap—planned scrap and unplanned scrap. Planned scrap is a normal part of the manufacturing process. If you were punching round holes out of a square piece of metal, there would be metal left over. This is planned scrap. (In the value analysis step of our process, we will look at reducing material costs.) (See page 68.) Unplanned scrap includes all the errors and mistakes made by the employees during the manufacturing process. Generally, unplanned scrap is included as part of indirect factory costs.

Planned scrap must be included under direct material costs. The buyer should figure how much material is normally left over after the product is made. The buyer then multiplies this number by the price of scrap to determine the value of this scrap. This value is subtracted from the gross direct material costs to determine net direct material costs.

In summary, direct material costs are determined by making out a bill of material (how much material), multiplying by prices (what does it cost), and subtracting scrap value.

## Determining Direct Labor Costs

To determine direct labor costs the buyer must again determine two things: how much labor is required and what it costs.

To determine how much labor is required, the buyer should meet with industrial engineering, manufacturing engineering, and other technical groups. They will have standard tables that tell how much time a factory operation takes. Time and motion studies have been published that provide detail concerning direct labor time values to the .001th of an hour. A good way to acquire knowledge of the exact manufacturing process is for the buyer to take a tour of the supplier's plant. A few hours' watching and learning about the process will save much time and make this step much more accurate.

To determine the labor costs, the buyer has many sources of information. Many labor contracts are public record. In these cases, the buyer can get actual labor rates. Many area chambers of commerce maintain information on area wage rates, which could be used for the area in which the supplier's plant is located. The federal government also publishes many statistics concerning labor costs.

The tolerance for amount of labor should be ± three percent, and the tolerance for what it costs should be ± one percent. Once the buyer has determined direct material costs and direct labor costs, these are added together to get *direct costs*.

## Determining Indirect Factory Costs

To determine indirect factory costs, the buyer must analyze all available information concerning the supplier (annual reports, Dun & Bradstreet's, etc.). There is usually a direct relationship between investment and indirect factory costs. The higher the investment, the more the indirect costs. A simple assembly operation does not need a lot of complicated equipment and setup employees and costs will be low. A highly complex product, requiring complex equipment, needs more maintenance and setup employees. Very complicated machines are much harder to maintain. If the buyer has no other information, he or she can use this table.

1. *Low Investment Industry.*   Indirect factory costs = direct labor costs

2. *Medium Investment Industry.*   Indirect factory costs = twice direct labor costs

3. *High Investment Industry.*   Indirect factory costs = three times direct labor costs

4. *High Investment and Complex Product.*   Indirect factory costs = four times direct labor costs

## Determining Indirect Office Costs

Again the buyer must generally use a ratio to determine these costs. They are most difficult to figure out. The buyer can use the information that follows. (Remember, product cost or the factory cost is the sum of direct material costs, direct labor costs, and indirect factory costs.)

Generally, there is a close relationship between investment and indirect office costs. A simple product does not require a lot of engineering talent to design it or purchasing talent to buy the items for it. An assembly line operation typically uses many of the same items. There are fewer bills to pay, so the accounting department can be small. However, the more complex the product or the more investment required to produce the product, the more people are needed in the office area to support production.

If the buyer takes a plant tour, he or she can get a feel for the size of the office force. It would be unrealistic to expect this tour to yield exact numbers. Therefore, the following table is a simple and effective way of determining indirect office costs. To start with, if the buyer has no other information, he or she should use the midpoint of the range. As the buyer uses this technique, he or she will be able to refine the percentage.

1. *Low Investment Industry.* Indirect office costs = 10%–15% of product costs
2. *Medium Investment Industry.* Indirect office costs = 15%–25% of product costs
3. *High Investment Industry.* Indirect office costs = 20%–35% of product costs
4. *High Investment and Complex Product.* Indirect office costs = 25%–45% of product costs

## Determining Profit

From the negotiating standpoint, profit is an element of cost to the buyer. This must be included when a cost analysis is completed. Profit and risk are directly related. The higher the risk, the higher the profit should be. When a high-risk project fails, no profit is realized. So high-risk businesses must generate high profit on projects that succeed so the total company will not go bankrupt.

Everyone would agree that producing pencils is a much lower-risk industry than producing children's toys. (How many hula-hoops were being produced in 1983?) You should use this table that relates risk to profit (total cost is the sum of direct material costs, direct labor costs, indirect factory costs, and indirect office costs).

1. **Low Risk Industry.**   Profit = 4%–8% of total cost
2. **Medium Risk Industry.**   Profit = 6%–12% of total cost
3. **High Risk Industry.**   Profit = 9%–18% of total cost

## Negotiate

The third step in the cost analysis procedure of a negotiation is for the buyer and seller to sit down and compare each element and to negotiate what will be allowed.

A very important part of this negotiation is "value analysis." Based upon the buyer's knowledge of the industry and/or product, the buyer should be able to suggest changes in the ordering process for materials and sources. Not only might such suggestions lower material costs, but may also lower indirect office costs and profit costs. There is a tremendous impact whenever material costs are reduced. At the same time, the buyer's technical people will be able to suggest alternate materials, production processes, tool changes, and so forth. Even if a specific suggestion is not accepted, a variation on it might be implemented. All improvements suggested should result in the buyer being in a stronger position to get reduced prices.

Many people do not fully realize the impact of material cost reductions. The following example will demonstrate this. (In most industries, material is about 40–60 percent of total price.)

A.  Current status—widget

| | |
|---|---|
| Direct material | $4.00 |
| Direct labor | 1.00 |
| Indirect factory (100%) | 1.00 |
| Indirect office (15%) | .90 |
| Profit (10%) | .69 |
| Price | $7.59 |

B.  New Status—10% Material Reduction

| | |
|---|---|
| Direct material | $3.60 |
| Direct labor | 1.00 |
| Indirect labor | 1.00 |
| Indirect office | .84 |
| Profit | .64 |
| Price | $7.08 |

This simple example shows that a 10 percent direct material cost reduction ($.40) will result in a larger price savings of $.51. Because of
the compounding, the total savings increased $.11 more (27 percent).

This effect is the same for labor. (Labor costs generally are a
smaller percentage of price and agreed reductions in them are
harder to achieve.) A direct labor reduction affects three other cost
areas: indirect factory, indirect office, and profit.

All professional negotiators in buying-selling negotiations must be
able to effectively use the cost analysis style of negotiation.

## CHECKPOINT 12: ANALYZE THE OTHER INFLUENCES

At this stage in planning a negotiation you should analyze the third
parties, the outside pressures, and the other influences that could affect the outcome of the negotiation. These may influence your side
of the table your opponent's side of the table, or both. But they will
affect the negotiation.

This review should include, but not be limited to answering the
following questions.

1. How will the current market conditions affect this negotiation?
2. Will any laws, regulations, and so forth affect this negotiation?
3. Will any government action affect this negotiation?
4. Will any action by your competitor's affect this negotiation?
5. Are there any materials or supplies in short supply that will affect this negotiation?

6. How will the inflation rate affect this negotiation?
7. Will an action or possible action by a foreign nation affect this negotiation?
8. Will the stock market affect this negotiation?
9. Will an upcoming political election affect this negotiation?
10. Will an upcoming union election affect this negotiation?
11. Will any personal problems affect this negotiation?

In sum, what could influence the negotiation that will not be at the negotiation table? How to take advantage of this information must be addressed during the planning of any negotiation.

## CHECKPOINT 13: EVALUATE YOUR POSITION

During the last four checkpoints you have analyzed your opponent's side, your opponent, the product, and the outside influences. This data should now allow you to evaluate your position relative to the opponent's. You must decide whether you are weak or strong as compared with your opponent. On the MAP form in the upper left-hand corner is an area to fill in one of the following descriptions of your position: (See Figure 4-14.)

1. Overwhelmingly strong
2. Extremely strong
3. Very strong
4. Strong
5. Slightly strong
6. Even
7. Slightly weak
8. Weak
9. Very weak
10. Extremely weak
11. Overwhelmingly weak

Strong / Position

Signature _a. m. Born_

| | (1) | (2) | (3) | (4) | (5) | (6) | (7) | (8) | (9) | (10) | (11) | (12) | (13) | (14) | (15) | (16) |
|---|---|---|---|---|---|---|---|---|---|---|---|---|---|---|---|---|
| | Issues | Type | $V_M$ | $V_{MR}$ | $V_{OR}$ | $V_O$ | Authority Limit | Information | | | | | | | | |
| Cash Terms | | W | 1% = $2,700 | | | 1% = $2,700 | Net in 30 days | 2 | | | | 1% in 10 days | | | | |
| | | | | | | | | | | | | | | | | |
| | | | | | | | | | | | | | | | | |
| | | | | | | | | | | | | | | | | |
| Avoid Issues | | | | | | | | | | | | | | | | |
| Lead Time | | — | $5,000/ week | | | $10,000/ week | Max 13 weeks | 7 | | | | 13 weeks | | | | |

FIGURE 4-14  MAP

71

Be realistic. If you are too optimistic or too pessimistic, you will hurt your chances of success. *Be honest.* This decision is key, because it will affect the balance of the planning process.

All of the previous 12 checkpoints have helped develop the data base from which you can objectively evaluate your position. You will make a mistake if you try to evaluate your position before this stage in the planning process. The work on the next five checkpoints will be based upon your strength in a particular negotiation.

## Beware of the Halo Effect

It is very possible that one week you will be in a negotiation in which your position is extremely strong and the next week be in a negotiation in which your position is very weak. Each negotiation is different. You must be aware of and guard against the "halo effect." To avoid it, you must make an independent evaluation each time you plan. The halo effect means that if most items look good, or if in most negotiations you are strong, then you will *believe* that all items are good or you are always strong. The halo effect arises from past items influencing current items, or a majority of items influencing all items, and so forth.

To avoid the halo effect, it is most important that each negotiation is evaluated independently.

## CHECKPOINT 14: PLAN YOUR AGENDA

At this stage in your planning you should decide the order in which you want to negotiate the issues to be negotiated. Of course you want the most advantageous order. There are several factors to consider in planning your agenda.

First consider several alternatives. You might do this by writing each issue or area of issues on a small card. Then move the cards around on your desk so that you can consider many different agendas without having to write out each possibility. Some people would call this "storyboarding." You must be as creative as possible. Remember the more potential alternatives you consider, the greater your probability of success. (Read a book on creativity. See Chapter 12.)

Second, do not become predictable. This is fatal in negotiations. Sellers tell me that there are five percent buyers, seven percent buyers, ten percent buyers, and so forth. That is, a buyer will expect to get a five percent concession during the negotiation, that is, a five percent buyer. Once you fall into a pattern you will always lose. The seller's strategy for a five percent buyer is to quote a price seven percent higher than the price at which the seller wants to sell. During the negotiation the seller will be "out negotiated" and reduce his or her price by five percent. The other two percent is for the seller's "trouble."

Some good friends of mine have always lived on a small farm in Ohio. They enjoy telling the story about the city slicker who purchased a farm in the area because the person wanted to "return to nature." After the first year the person had lost a large sum of money. The person could not understand why and was talking to a neighbor. The city slicker said, "Do you know I spent $10,000 last year just for electricity?" The neighbor could not believe it. The city slicker said, "It costs a lot to keep the electric fence in operation all the time." The neighbor laughed and laughed and said, "You don't have to keep it on all the time. Cows are very predictable. Once they learn the fence is 'hot' they stay away from it." I hope that in the future your actions are not like those of a predictable cow, but like an unpredictable negotiations professional.

Third, you should plan answers and directions when your opponent reacts to a proposal. For example, suppose a union negotiator plans to ask for an eight percent raise? What happens if management says no? The union negotiator should know what to say next. What happens if management says yes? Maybe management was prepared to give 10 percent. The union negotiator better have a sentence ready to try to get more. This is very much like writing a flowchart for a computer software program.

Fourth, in a negotiation the agenda plan is essential. You have the option of quickly going over each issue to be negotiated to see if you can get a quick agreement on a few of the issues. Another option is to negotiate one issue at a time. Another option is to send a copy of the agenda to your opponent for comment, and revise the agenda. A fourth option is to discuss the minor parts first and save the "battle" until later. Whatever the option, make it the best for you.

My personal style is to include a few of my give points first on the agenda. It is a fact that early issues discussed in a negotiation, or in any meeting for that matter, tend to be scrutinized very carefully. People want to start off on the right foot. People generally adhere to the poker player's philosophy that if you do not win with the first pot, you can not win them all. Therefore, I like to start a negotiation with issues I know I will lose. I like to let my opponent work hard at winning, while I relax. This provides two advantages. First, for the rest of the negotiation my opponent will be more tired than I am. Second, my opponent will have IOUs on his or her side of the table (issues the person has won) that I will try to cash in later in the negotiation to win issues I must have.

As a negotiation or meeting progresses people tend to become frustrated and want to end it. Most people like to negotiate very rapidly, especially in our culture. Toward the end of a negotiation an opponent is likely to give a little more than early on, in order to get agreement and end the process. Therefore, it may be advantageous to have more important issues later in your agenda.

A final factor is Figure 4-15. This plots the number of agreements versus time in negotiation. Most agreements occur at the end of a negotiation. Of course, this is my personal style and I work hard at

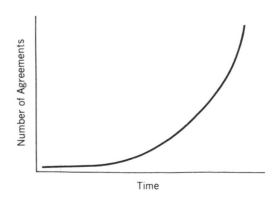

**FIGURE 4-15**  Agreement versus time in negotiation

Strong / Position  A. M. Born / Signature

| (1) Issues | (2) Type | (3) $V_M$ | (4) $V_{MR}$ | (5) $V_{OR}$ | (6) $V_O$ | (7) Authority Limit | (8) Information | (9) Agenda | (10) | (11) | (12) $O_O$ | (13) | (14) | (15) | (16) |
|---|---|---|---|---|---|---|---|---|---|---|---|---|---|---|---|
| Cash Terms | W | 1% = $2,700 | | | 1% = $2,700 | Net 30 days | 2 | 3 | | | 1% in 10 days | | | | |
| Avoid Issues / Lead Time | — | $5,000/ week | | | $10,000/ week | Max 13 weeks | 7 | — | | | 13 weeks | | | | |

**FIGURE 4-16** MAP

75

not being predictable. You may also be successful using this approach.

Also, do not forget that you will often negotiate again with the opponent and the opponent's company. Perhaps in your plan for one negotiation you can discuss an issue so that you can win that issue in your next negotiation.

Once you have decided upon an agenda, use column 9 in your MAP to list the order of the issues to be negotiated. (See Figure 4-16)

## CHECKPOINT 15: WRITE OUT YOUR QUESTIONS

A truism of most negotiations is that the side that asks the most questions usually wins and the side that answers the most questions usually loses. This relates to another truism—that the side that talks the most generally loses.

Writing out your questions is an ongoing step in the planning process. During the planning it is helpful to keep a separate sheet of paper to write down the questions you want to have answered during the negotiation. Generally we have so much on our minds when we plan a negotiation that it is very easy to forget a question we wanted to ask. So write them down.

There are several purposes for questions. The first purpose is to test assumptions. In Checkpoint 8, collecting facts was reviewed. It was suggested that assumptions be marked with a special symbol. It is also suggested that you write one or more questions that you can use during the actual negotiation to determine whether your assumption is true.

The second purpose of questions, which is self-evident, is to get information.

A third purpose of questions is to give information. For example, assume you arrive at your office one hour late and meet your boss. Your boss asks, "Do you know what time it is?" Your boss knows the time, but is using a question to *give* the information that you are late.

Sellers, of course, use questions to bring a negotiation, or section of a negotiation, to a conclusion. For example, they may ask, "At this price, may I write your order?" "Can we agree that these will be the terms and conditions of this proposed contract?"

Questions can also get attention: "Are you ready to negotiate?"

Finally, questions can be used to "get you off the hook." These are relay or reverse questions. They are very useful in negotiations. (They also are very useful in teaching.) A relay question is one that you ask another person to answer a question that is addressed to you. There is a right way and a wrong way to relay a question. During the thousand of negotiation case studies and role plays that I have observed, I have seen the *wrong* way used many, many times. For example, the salesperson will ask the buyer, "How much will be saved if the tolerances on the drawings are changed from .005 to .010?" The buyer has no idea so the buyer says, "Engineer, answer that question." The look on the engineer's face is one of complete panic. The engineer mumbles something and sometimes gives a false answer or an answer that hurts the buyer's and engineer's team. This is the *wrong way* to relay a question. You must *not* put your team member on the spot. This will make your team member look bad, will adversely affect your team position, and may even make the team member your enemy.

The correct way to relay a question is to give your team member a chance to think about the answer before asking that person to answer the question. In the example given the correct way to relay the question is for the buyer to say, "Seller, I believe that the engineer is the most qualified person to answer your question concerning the tolerance on drawings, but before I ask the engineer to answer the question, let me make sure that I understand it. You asked, 'How much will be saved if the tolerances on the drawings are changed from .005 to .010?' Is that correct?" The seller must now respond "Yes." The buyer can then say, "Engineer, will you please answer this question: How much will be saved if the tolerances on the drawings are changed from .005 to .010?" This procedure buys you time. It allows your team member to think about the answer. First, you alert your team member that you plan to relay the question to him or her. ("I believe that the engineer is the most qualified person"), and second, you give the team member time by repeating the question at least twice and by getting your opponent to reconfirm the question. This is significantly better than saying, "Here's the engineer." Giving your team member time to think is the *right way* to relay a question.

The reverse question is simply giving the question back to your opponent. For example, by asking, "How much do you think will be saved by changing the tolerances on the drawings from .005 to .010?"

A seminar participant once told me that he started off *every* negotiation by stating, "I have a list of questions and I will not negotiate until I get satisfactory answers to each of these questions." This may not be a bad idea at times, but since the person does it every time, I am sure it hurts. (See Checkpoint 14 about being predictable.) However, you must have a list of questions that you plan to ask during the actual negotiation. This is the only way to absolutely assure that you do not forget anything.

How many times have you, shortly after a negotiation, meeting, course, and so forth, said to yourself, "I forgot to ask XXXX," or "I didn't find out about YYYY, or I'll have to call Mr. ZZZZ." All of us have experienced this frustration. The best way to avoid the frustration is to *write* down every question as soon as you think about it and to be sure to *ask* every question during the negotiation.

Some people believe that asking questions is a sign of weakness or of not being very smart. This is absolutely false. The professional negotiator understands that it is impossible for any person to know everything. The professional also knows that the purpose of the negotiation is to get the best deal for the principal. So the professional will ask any question that will help obtain the principal's objectives. You should feel the same way.

## CHECKPOINT 16: DETERMINE INITIAL POSITIONS

One of the more important steps in the planning process is determining your initial position on each issue to be negotiated. Where will you start? In Chapter 2 we reviewed the negotiations diagram. You will recall that each side (buyer, seller, management, labor, etc.) established a position at the start of the negotiation. This was not the position at which they expected to reach agreement. It was just a starting point. Hundreds of case studies have proven that the side that gives itself the most movement gives itself an advantage in the actual negotiation.

In column 10 of the MAP (Figure 4-17) you should write your initial position (IPm) for each issue to be negotiated. (In Checkpoint 17

a. m. Bou / Signature

| | (1) Issues | (2) Type | (3) $V_M$ | (4) $V_{MR}$ | (5) $V_{OR}$ | (6) $V_O$ | (7) Authority Limit | (8) Information | (9) Agenda | (10) $I_{PM}$ | (11) | (12) $O_O$ | (13) | (14) | (15) | (16) |
|---|---|---|---|---|---|---|---|---|---|---|---|---|---|---|---|---|
| Cash Terms | | W | 1% = $2,700 | | | 1% = $2,700 | Net in 30 days | 2 | 3 | 3% in 30 days | | 1% in 10 days | | | | |
| Avoid Issues / Lead Time | | — | $5,000/ week | | | $10,000/ week | Max 13 weeks | 7 | — | — | | 13 weeks | | | | |

**FIGURE 4-17** MAP

you will be asked to put your objectives in column 11.) At this check-point you should decide where you will start and how you plan to "give in." Major considerations are the rate, the size of the concessions, and the number of steps between your initial position and objective. This is one of two checkpoints that deal primarily with strategies and tactics during the negotiation. In Checkpoint 18 strategies and tactics will be reviewed. These checkpoints will complete our "game plan."

In column 13 of the MAP (Figure 4-18) you should note what position you think the opposition will initially take (IPo) on each issue to be negotiated. You must also complete this checkpoint for the issues to be avoided. It is very likely that your opponent will bring your weak points into the negotiation.

Everyone will agree that the tolerance on IPm (Initial position—me) will be zero. Everyone will also agree that tolerance on IPo (Initial position—opponent) will not be zero. But that is all right. It is most important that you think through where you believe your opponent will start.

In many negotiations IPo will be a known. For example, many times a buyer will have a quotation from the potential supplier that the buyer plans to negotiate with. Or management might have a list of "demands" from labor. You should be cautioned that at the start of the actual negotiation the IPo might be changed by your opponent.

A perfect example once happened in one of my standard case studies. The following is the important data given to both sides:

The Tremendous Turbine Company is the sole source for auxiliary turbine drive assemblies. Stover Steam asked for prices for four units (with an option for six more units) and requested a meeting to review the quotation and the "relationship between the companies." Serious problems have occurred as shown in the recent history of these assemblies.

1. Eighteen months ago a six-unit order was placed at a firm price of $109,000/unit (DEST/ALLOWED) with delivery in 15 months.

2. Approximately a year ago the president of Tremendous asked for help in the form of an "adjustment" due to inflation of 10

Strong Position

Signature — A. M. Born

| (1) Issues | (2) Type | (3) $V_M$ | (4) $V_{MR}$ | (5) $V_{OR}$ | (6) $V_O$ | (7) Authority Limit | (8) Information | (9) Agenda | (10) $IP_M$ | (11) | (12) $O_O$ | (13) $IP_O$ | (14) | (15) | (16) |
|---|---|---|---|---|---|---|---|---|---|---|---|---|---|---|---|
| Cash Terms | W | 1% = $2,700 | | | 1% = $2,700 | Net 30 days | 2 | 3 | 3% in 30 days | | 1% in 10 days | Net in 30 days | | | |
| | | | | | | | | | | | | | | | |
| | | | | | | | | | | | | | | | |
| | | | | | | | | | | | | | | | |
| Avoid Issues | | | | | | | | | | | | | | | |
| Lead Time | — | $5,000/ week | | | $10,000/ week | Max 13 weeks | 7 | — | — | | 13 weeks | 27 weeks | | | |

**FIGURE 4-18**  MAP

81

percent. After several hours of negotiation at the Stover Steam office, Stover reluctantly agreed, but received a firm price of $120,000.

3. Six months later the Tremendous salesperson notified Stover that the six-unit order would be late.

4. Last month the salesperson called and said, "We will ship next month if you agree to a price of $127,000."

5. The new quote (per unit) for four units is as follows (FOB factory) with a lead time of 14 months:

| | |
|---|---:|
| Raw materials | $ 60,000 |
| Purchased parts | 12,700 |
| Labor | 38,500 |
| | 111,200 |
| | |
| General & administrative expenses | 11,120 |
| | 122,320 |
| | |
| Profit | 12,232 |
| | $134,552 |

In the confidential information that is given to the buyers (Stover Steam) some of the data is:

1. The legal department reviewed your order for the six units and advised that the current contract at $120,000 is airtight. Tremendous has no legal basis to withhold shipment.

2. You have attempted to develop an in-company source for these assemblies, but they want $250,000 "development" costs.

3. Recently you sent requests for quotations to "anybody and everybody," but so far no one has indicated a desire to make these assemblies because of the very tight drawing tolerances.

4. Last week the buyer's son, who is a caddie at the local country club, saw the president of Tremendous playing golf as a partner with your division engineering manager.

In the confidential information that is given to the seller (Tremendous Turbine) some of the data is:

1. Your lawyer stated that if Stover goes to court (it will be at least a year before the hearing), they will hold you to $120,000. Your $127,000 quotation is just a give point so that you can get $134,553 on all new orders. You plan to give in after a "long hard battle."
2. Your president is a very good friend of the Stover engineering manager. This has resulted in tolerances on drawings that only your company can meet. As a matter of fact, last week they played golf together during his "secret" trip to town.

During the planning sessions the buyers really talked "tough." Statements such as the following were made: "We've got them—let's not let them off the hook"; "They are trying to blackmail us; we must stop that fast"; "We are very, very strong"; "The best action is to sue."

Finally, the buyers decided that their strategy would be not to negotiate anything, until Tremendous agrees that the old order will be shipped at $120,000. They also decided that "$134,552 for the new order was much too high and that, because of the learning curve, the new price should be about the same as the old price of $120,000."

When the negotiation started both sides introduced themselves. Then the person acting as the president of Tremendous stood up and said, "I'm very sorry, but a major mistake was made. Our estimating department made some mathematical errors. Here is a new quote (per unit) for four units.

| | |
|---|---:|
| Raw materials | $ 64,270 |
| Purchased parts | 14,900 |
| Labor | 38,500 |
| | 118,670 |
| General and administrative | 11,867 |
| | 130,537 |
| Profit | 13,053 |
| | $143,590 |

This mistake is the responsibility of the marketing department. I have fired our marketing manager. I can do nothing else except say I am very sorry. But remember, our price is $143,590."

What happened in this case was that the sellers used a negotiation tactic called "negative concession" (i.e., they moved away from the other side) and changed their initial position. This took the buying team completely by surprise. It knocked the wind out of their sails and they lost all their fight. In this case study the contract was signed at $120,000 for the old units and $141,000 for the new. The sellers completely won the case.

This is an example that illustrates how the prenegotiation quote and the IPo may be different at the start of a negotiation. A good planner will consider this alternative.

In many cases you don't have an indication of IPo, so you must look at the negotiation from your opponent's viewpoint. Review the information discussed in Checkpoints 9, 10, and 12. Then fill in column 13 of the MAP. You will probably be within five percent of your opponent's real numbers. The most important thing is that you go through that process. Columns 10 and 13 of the MAP now establish the extremes of the negotiation. Somewhere between these two positions a settlement could be accomplished.

## CHECKPOINT 17: ESTABLISH YOUR OBJECTIVES

This is the most important checkpoint of all, because it is a truism of the negotiation process that you *never get more than you ask for in negotiations*. A second truism is that if you *cannot measure an objective it isn't worth a damn*.

In a negotiation seminar I have conducted for several years, the class is organized so that half the class are buyers and half are sellers. There are five complicated role-play case studies in which class members act as buyers and sellers. The opening case study concerns buying a car. Both buyers and sellers are given the following information.

Two weeks ago the buyer visited the Honest Abe Auto Agency. The buyer discussed several models with the sales manager. One model (Super Sport Two) was of most interest. It had the following specifications:

Engine: V-6 245 in³

Doors: 2

Trunk: 18 ft³

Color: white/red roof

Tires: steel-belted radials with rally wheels

Power steering/power brakes/air conditioning/AM radio

Mileage rating: 18 city/25 road

Part of the negotiation is the trade-in of a three-year old sedan. When the buyer first visited he was given a value of $2,270 for his trade-in. The sticker price of Super Sport Two is $7,950. Also discussed was the fact that the interest rate on a loan from Honest Abe would be 9.6 percent per year. The buyer has just arrived at Honest Abe's two weeks later.

The buyers in the class are given the following confidential information: You have a major problem or two. First, the car you are trading in has a very serious crack in the block. You believe that the dealer has not yet spotted it. Your gas station mechanic said, "Get rid of it as fast as possible; it may not go another 100 miles." Second, your spouse really likes Super Sport Two. You visited several other dealers during the past week and *nothing* would satisfy your spouse. Third, you have $1,000 you could put toward the purchase of a car, but the balance (price less trade) must be financed. Your bank quoted 9.2 percent for a three-year loan, but would not give you the money because of the other outstanding loans you have with them.

According to the "blue book" your current car retails for $2,340–$2,490 (according to the condition of the car). Your spouse is not with you. You both agreed that you must buy a car today. The sales manager does not know that you can make a purchase commitment.

Write here your objective for the purchase price _____.

Write here your actual purchase price _____.

The sellers are also given a sheet that contains confidential information: You have a major problem or two. First, today is the last day of your yearly bonus period. If you can sell one more car you qualify for a trip to Europe, with your spouse, for three weeks. This is your last "hot" prospect of the day. Second, the margin on the car the buyer wants is small. If you could sell him the following car (Regular Sport Six) your company would make much more profit.

Engine: V-8 305 in³

Doors: 2

Trunk: 16 ft³

Color: red/white roof

Tires: steel-belted radials, rally wheels

Power steering/power brakes, air conditioning, AM/FM stereo radio

Mileage Rating: 16 city/27 road

Sticker price: $8,809.

Since the president is out of town you have complete authority to make any deal you are satisfied with. (The buyer does not know of the president's absence.) Your invoice cost for Super Two is $6,027. Your invoice cost for Regular Sport Six is $6,372. You know that you can sell the trade-in for $2,007 on the wholesale market. Its retail value is approximately $2,350.

You quoted a little high on the rate of interest for the loan as a give point in the negotiation that will hopefully take the buyer's mind off the price. You get money from the local bank at 9.2 percent, plus you get a commission of $500 for every loan you "sell." This commission goes into your pocket.

Write here your objective for the selling price ———————————.

Write here the actual selling price ———————————————.

The class is paired off so that one buyer will negotiate with one seller. Generally there will be 12–15 negotiations all going on at the same time. Each person is given 40 minutes to plan negotiation strategy. They are told not to use too many "sky hooks." After 40 minutes the buyers and sellers "meet," shake hands, and start one-on-one negotiations. They are told the negotiations will last one hour and that the car *must* be bought and sold. They do not have the option to break off negotiations, since the car must be sold. The case is written so that the variable is the buyer's price objective.

Before the negotiations start each person's confidential sheet is checked to be sure the person has written down a price objective. When the negotiation is over, both the buyer and seller write down the actual price on their sheet and the sheets are turned in.

The variable is the buyer's objective. Since the sellers must sell, the buyer will say no until the actual price is near the buyer's objective. As the negotiations are in progress, pressure is put on the sellers by announcing that the sellers have $x$ minutes to sell the car.

For the critique of this case study an analysis is made comparing the various buyers' objectives to their actual prices. It always happens that the buyers who set low price objectives paid low prices and the buyers who set high objectives paid high prices. Here is an actual table of results (price less trade-in less $1000) from a recent seminar:

| Buyer's Objective | Actual Price |
|---|---|
| $4,000 | $4,150 |
| 4,000 | 4,190 |
| 4,200 | 4,670 |
| 4,300 | 4,790 |
| 4,490 | 4,820 |
| 4,500 | 5,000 |
| 4,700 | 4,900 |
| 5,000 | 5,260 |
| 5,200 | 5,450 |
| 5,200 | 5,510 |
| 5,400 | 5,800 |
| 5,500 | 5,750 |
| 5,550 | 5,930 |

With the exception of one pair the order in both columns is exactly the same. The buyer with the lowest objective paid the lowest price.

The buyer with the second lowest objective paid the second lowest price. The buyer with the highest objective paid the highest price.

Yes, it is true that not one of the buyers paid a price equal to the buyer's objective. (Again, see the negotiations diagram in Chapter 2.) But there was a very direct relationship between objectives and results. To repeat a truism of the negotiation process: you *never get more than you ask for in negotiations*. This is why this checkpoint is the most important of all 25 checkpoints.

Once a person achieves his or her objectives in a negotiation, he or she will relax. There is significantly less pressure to do better. If the person cannot relax, because the objective is not close, the pressure to do better remains.

Sports provide examples of this point that the objective of one team or individual affects the results. Great champions have a very strong desire to win. One example is the Super Bowl game in 1973 between the Washington Redskins (George Allen's "over the hill gang") and the Miami Dolphins. The year before Miami had lost the Super Bowl to Dallas. During the two weeks before the game much of the information coming out of the Washington training camp indicated the team thought it was great that the over the hill gang was in the Super Bowl, that the old men of the league were conference champions. At the same time the information from the Miami camp indicated the team's attitude was we will not lose again. I believe that at the start of the game the Washington team's objective had been met. They were in the Super Bowl. But the objective of Miami—win the Super Bowl—had not been met. This had a major impact on the game, which Miami won.

Another example is the November, 1966, football game between Notre Dame and Michigan State Universities. This was the game of the year, the game of the decade, and, some said, the game of the century. Notre Dame was ranked first and Michigan State second. The score was tied 10–10 late in the game. Notre Dame had the ball in fairly good field position. Instead of trying to win, the Irish played for a tie. They ran the ball into the middle of the line. They did not try any play designed to gain a lot of yards at a higher risk. In fact Notre Dame did not try to win (just to do their best). Most football fans were shocked. Notre Dame—the most famous of all college football teams—played for a tie. The front cover of the November 28,

1966 issue of *Sports Illustrated* showed one of the final plays of the game—a Notre Dame running play. Eight years later I heard the announcer at the 1974 Sugar Bowl game between Notre Dame and Alabama say, when Notre Dame completed a pass from their own end zone (a very high risk play), "I hope this proves to America that Ara Parsegian doesn't always play for a tie." Eight years after Notre Dame settled for less than the best, that earlier game was still in the minds of football fans. The important point is that if you settle for less than your best, others may be upset. More importantly, *you* should be upset.

During this checkpoint, fill in on the MAP Column 11 (Om) with your objectives (Figure 4-19), in dollars and cents (every issue to be negotiated can be resolved into dollars and cents). You may also wish to review Checkpoint 5. In doing this step of the planning remember two points: (1) You never get more than you ask for in negotiations; (2) If you cannot measure an objective it isn't worth a damn.

## CHECKPOINT 18: DETERMINE STRATEGIES AND TACTICS

Column 14 of the MAP (Figure 4-20) should be used to list the strategy or tactic that is planned for winning each point.

Many books have been written (see the list in Chapter 12) that describe the hundreds of strategies and tactics used in negotiations. A few examples will demonstrate the wide range available to any negotiator.

### Lower than the Boss

In this tactic the negotiator states that he or she will accept less from the opponent to reach an agreement that the boss wants. A buyer might say to a seller, "Yesterday my boss told me I should be able to get your company to cut 10 percent from the quoted price. But I know you will give good service and good quality and I want to buy from you, so I'll accept a cut of only 7.5 percent." Hopefully the seller will believe that he or she is getting a good deal and "saving" 2.5 percent of the quoted price. Also the buyer can tell the seller, "If we don't

Strong / Position

a. m. Born
Signature

| | ① Issues | ② Type | ③ $V_M$ | ④ $V_{MR}$ | ⑤ $V_{OR}$ | ⑥ $V_O$ | ⑦ Authority Limit | ⑧ Information | ⑨ Agenda | ⑩ $IP_M$ | ⑪ $O_M$ | ⑫ $O_O$ | ⑬ $IP_O$ | ⑭ | ⑮ | ⑯ |
|---|---|---|---|---|---|---|---|---|---|---|---|---|---|---|---|---|
| Cash Terms | | W | 1% = $2,700 | | | 1% = $2,700 | Net 30 days | 2 | 3 | 3% in 30 days | 2% in 15 days | 1% in 10 days | Net in 30 days | | | |
| Avoid Issues / Lead Time | | — | $5,000/ week | | | $10,000/ week | Max 13 weeks | 7 | — | — | — | 13 weeks | 27 weeks | | | |

FIGURE 4-19 MAP

Strong / Position

a. M. Born / Signature

| (1) Issues | (2) Type | (3) $V_M$ | (4) $V_{MR}$ | (5) $V_{OR}$ | (6) $V_O$ | (7) Authority Limit | (8) Information | (9) Agenda | (10) $IP_M$ | (11) $O_M$ | (12) $O_O$ | (13) $IP_O$ | (14) Tactics | (15) | (16) |
|---|---|---|---|---|---|---|---|---|---|---|---|---|---|---|---|
| Cash Terms | W | 1% = $2,700 | | | 1% = $2,700 | Net 30 days | 2 | 3 | 3% in 30 days | 2% in 15 days | 1% in 10 days | Net in 30 days | Lower than the boss | | |
| Avoid Issues<br>Lead Time | — | $5,000/ week | | | $10,000/ week | Max 13 weeks | 7 | — | — | — | 13 weeks | 27 weeks | — | | |

**FIGURE 4-20**  MAP

91

reach agreement and my boss gets involved, it will cost you 2.5 percent so you had better reach agreement with me." Or the buyer can tell the seller, "I'm paying you a 2.5 percent premium, so you should give me issues x, y, and z."

A friend made extra money when selling a house by using a "lower than the husband" tactic. It is often assumed that the husband does all the negotiating when a house is bought and sold. In this case, the wife was the chief negotiator, although the buyers did not know this. The husband stated, "Based upon the costs of our new house, we must sell this house at X." When the sellers found a couple who was interested, the wife started negotiating with the wife. Her conversation went something like this: "Moving is a major problem, don't you agree? My husband is gone all week, returns home late Friday night, works around the house all day Saturday, sleeps most of Sunday, and returns to the new job Sunday night. He never spends time with the kids. I believe that kids should spend time with their fathers. Don't you agree? I want my kids to do that, so I'll accept 10 percent less for the house just to get my family back together." Since the other couple thought they were getting a special deal, they jumped, and agreed to a price 10 percent less than the asking price.

What makes this such a successful tactic is that the appraised value (the average of three appraisals) was 22 percent less than the asking price. Using this tactic enabled the sellers to make 12 percent extra profit on the sale of one house.

## Loaf of Bread

This is one of the oldest of all tactics: simply to ask for small increments, not large ones, during negotiations. For a buyer, this tactic suggests asking for 10 one-percent price reductions, not one 10-percent price reduction. It is much easier to give in in small amounts.

After discussing this tactic, a seminar participant told me that he now understood how he lost to his wife. He said, "On Monday morning, as I was leaving for work, my wife asked for $20 to pick up a couple of things. Tuesday morning it was another $20, yesterday it was $10, and this morning another $20. If she had said to me Sunday evening 'Give me $70 for odds and ends now, since I know you will be busy this week,' I would have said no. But a little each day was easy to say yes to."

In other types of negotiations the principle is the same. And this tactic can be used many times in the same negotiation.

## Comparative Options

This tactic allows the opponent to make a choice. You outline the options open for agreement, giving the opponent two options: one he or she cannot accept, and one that you want. Once the opponent has made the decision, he or she cannot complain about the outcome. During a negotiation you can use this tactic many times. Keep proposing different packages (another reason to have many give points), two at a time. In one package have something your opponent cannot accept and in the other package all items that are acceptable to you.

This tactic can be put to good use in family life. For example, a wife may say to her husband, "What do you want to do this weekend, go see my mother or go to a movie?" The husband does not want to see his mother-in-law so quickly replies, "Go see a movie" (a win for the wife). It is possible that at the movie there is a long line. When the husband gets angry the wife says, "You are the one who decided to go to the movie." She may even try another comparative option: "Of course, if you don't want to wait in line we could go out for dinner." A $10 movie has now become a $60 dinner. The wife may even try a third time. After an appetizer (with half a bottle of white wine) and a big salad and main course (with a bottle of red wine) she may say, "Dinner has been wonderful and we have had a lot to eat. We could have dessert or spend the same money going to the late show at the movie." Each time the wife gave two options, one the husband could not accept and the other one the wife wanted.

## If

This is another very old tactic to get the other side to make a commitment without making one yourself.

For example, a seller might say, "If we agree to pay the freight, will you give us the order?" If the buyer says yes, has the buyer made a commitment? There is no doubt the buyer has made a commitment. But the seller is not at all committed.

The seller has determined the conditions under which the buyer will place an order. The buyer is in a bad position. The seller could say, "Of course, you know that it is against company policy to pay freight, but I will ask my boss if she can bend policy on this order."

## Negative Concession

This tactic is based on the idea that you do not always have to move toward your opponent. Many times it is very effective to move away and have the opponent "chase" you.

Buying a car provides an example. The seller could use a negative concession with the value of your old car. When most people buy a car they look at a number of different dealers and do preliminary negotiations. At that time the seller may say, "Your trade-in is worth *x* dollars." After this first round the buyer usually picks two or three places to really negotiate. When these "final" negotiations start, the seller could take a "closer" look at the trade-in and say it is only worth 20 percent fewer dollars. This is a negative concession. The seller now has a number of alternatives: The 20 percent could be a give point at the end to "seal" the deal. The 20 percent could be used to get the buyer to add options to the value of the new car. Or the 20 percent could be used to get the buyer to upgrade to a higher-priced car. ("If you buy this deluxe model your trade-in could be valued at *x* dollars.") In any case, the seller is ahead.

## Association

This tactic pits the negotiators against their bosses and/or principals. A buyer might say to a seller, "If you can just cut the price one percent more, I can give you an order today and my boss will not get involved. If my boss gets into this negotiation, your boss will also get involved. They will complicate matters. It is so much easier to keep them out and have all business just between the two of us."

Labor negotiators could also use this tactic: "If you don't agree to give this small issue I will file a grievance. At that time your boss, personnel relations, and maybe even top management will get involved. It would be so much easier to just give this small issue."

## Silence

This tactic is simple. Do not say anything. Most people cannot stand silence. They will start talking after only a few seconds of silence. When they talk there is a possibility that they will give away some information or reveal a new position. For sellers, silence is very bad, so buyers are advised to use this tactic.

## Summary

Consider this question: "Is it okay to plan to trap your opponent during the planning stage of negotiations?" If "trap" means to lie, cheat, steal, prepare false data, and so forth, the answer is no. But if "trap" means to plan to use acceptable strategies and tactics during the negotiation, the answer is yes. It is all right to plan to trap your opponent, and all negotiations professionals accept that. Column 14 of the MAP (Figure 4-20) is a very important column. A negotiation planning job is not complete unless you have considered what tactics you will use to win, or lose (if that is the plan), each issue to be negotiated.

It is all right to use strategies and tactics during a negotiation.

Some believe otherwise. I suggest this is erroneous. The process of negotiation implies that strategies and tactics are a significant part of the process. To be successful in negotiations, the professional negotiator knows when to use the right strategy or tactic, as well as when *not* to use any strategies or tactics.

The point here is to prepare yourself to use the strategies and tactics you have planned, including what you will say, how you will say it, and so forth. This is almost like diagramming a play, and it is very serious.

## CHECKPOINT 19: ROLE-PLAY

If a picture is worth a thousand words, then one role-play will prevent thousands of mistakes. The essence of this checkpoint is to practice your negotiation.

Ask a peer or your boss to take the part of your opponent and practice the negotiation. Their purpose would be to find all of the weak points in your plan. They should play devil's advocate.

An even better idea would be to find a person who performs the same function as the person you will be negotiating with. For example, if you are a buyer, ask a seller in your company to role-play with you. In my experience, people in purchasing are good in taking the role of a buyer, but not very good as sellers because they approach the seller's position from a buyer's background. Their value system is not the same. The converse also holds true.

If this second approach is not possible, consider this idea. A friend of mine was a purchasing manager at a large plant in the Midwest that was planning the negotiation for the most important commodity they purchased. This one commodity accounted for nearly 14 percent of the plant's total purchases. There were eight buyers in the department at that time. The purchasing manager called all of them into the office and said something like this:

> *We have a very important negotiation scheduled for two months from now. Before we do our final planning I want to role-play the negotiation. You four buyers will form the purchasing team and you four buyers will form the sales team. [When the purchasing manager made these assignments, the manager did the key thing—putting the buyer who would actually negotiate with the company's supplier on the seller's team for this mock negotiation.] The role-play will take place in my office in two weeks. You can use any information you want. After the mock negotiation, which will last from 3:00–6:30 or so, we will have a cookout.*

During the two-week period the buyers worked hard preparing their respective sides.

The mock negotiation started at 3:00 P.M. and lasted until about 7:00 P.M. During the negotiation the purchasing manager took very complete notes. When the manager felt the objective of the role-play had been accomplished, he stopped the mock negotiation. The manager collected all the information from the buyer's side of this role-play, and gave it to the buyer who would conduct the actual negotiation. The manager then picked up all the information from the seller's side of the role-play and gave it to the buyer. Finally, the manager gave the buyer all of the notes he had taken. The manager said, "With all of this data you can now plan your real strategy."

Because the buyer, who was on the sales team, gained insights that he did not have before the mock negotiation, he was better able to prepare his strategy for the actual negotiation.

The results of the actual negotiation, six weeks later, was a tremendous cost reduction for the buyer's company. After the results were documented and finalized, the purchasing manager called me. (The purchasing manager and the buyers were former seminar students.) We discussed in detail how they were able to save so much money.

Then the purchasing manager gave the "bottom line": a month after the purchase order was placed and everything taken care of, the buyer came into the purchasing manager's office and said, "I'm going to quit." The manager said, "Why? You are a hero! Everyone from the janitor to the general manager knows that you saved our company lots of money. Your picture will be on the front page of our company newspaper. Why do you want to quit?" The buyer said, "I want to go to work for the company I just negotiated with. If the team that negotiated with me is their best, I'll be their top salesperson in one year, district manager in two years, and vice-president of sales in less than three years. On this issue in the negotiation they made a bad presentation, on this issue their logic was poor, and they forgot this issue." What had happened was the buyer knew more about the sales side of the negotiation than the sellers did. Because of the mock negotiation the buyer was better prepared to negotiate the sales position than the seller's people were.

How would you like to negotiate with someone who knew more about your side of the table than you? It would be very, very difficult. The point of this type of role-play is to prepare yourself from the opponent's point of view.

It is true that role-plays generate a lot of enthusiasm and contribute to building a team. Those in the role-play generally exert themselves to prepare the case because they want to look good in front of their peers and as a result they learn a lot about the process of negotiation. We cannot practice too much.

Another technique is to videotape your role-plays. Then you can rerun them, have instant replays, and catch your mistakes. Today, this does not cost very much. Watching a tape of your mock negotiation is a powerful teaching device.

Practice! Practice! Practice! is a very serious checkpoint. Even a sin-

gle practice session will help you when you get into the actual negotiation.

## CHECKPOINT 20: REVISE YOUR PLAN

During this checkpoint you revise your plan as a result of the mock
negotiation.

Your opponent in the mock negotiation will have worked hard at
making you look bad. That person will try to find all the holes in your
plan. Your opponent will also ask many hard questions and take positions that cannot be supported by logic. All of this behavior is based
upon the desire to help you prepare your final plan.

At this stage in the process, you address all the problems that sur-
faced during the mock negotiation. This gives you an opportunity to
revise your plan, restructure your strategies, develop a new agenda,
and so forth. The value of the mock negotiation is threefold:

1.   An opportunity to complete the experience of the real negotia-
     tion.
2.   An opportunity to discover many of the problems in your orig-
     inal plan.
3.   And, most important, an opportunity to revise and improve your
     plan.

It does not require a lot to describe this checkpoint, but it is a very
important one.

## CHECKPOINT 21: WHERE AND WHEN
## TO NEGOTIATE

This checkpoint covers the where and when decisions concerning the
negotiation, as well as other related administrative matters.

### Location

There are three possible sites for conducting a negotiation: (1) your
location, (2) your opponent's location, or (3) a neutral location. Each

has pros and cons, which a negotiator should review to make the most advantageous decision.

## Your Location

There are many advantages. It is your home turf. In your office, you are the boss. In your office you can control interruptions, the seating arrangement, the temperature, and so forth. You have a psychological edge. The opponent is the visitor, is generally not comfortable, and usually must leave at a certain time. At your location, you have all of the resources available to get any piece of data you need. You can call in experts whenever they are needed. Having the negotiation at your location is the least disruptive to your normal routine.

## Your Opponent's Location

There are also many advantages to this location. First, if your opponent uses the tactic—"I'll have to check back at the office"—to get out of trouble, you can say, "Let's go to that department and get the answer right now." At your opponent's location the opponent cannot use this tactic. Second, at the opponent's place you have the opportunity to escalate the level of the negotiation. You can try to bring your opponent's boss into the negotiation, or the boss's boss if it will help you. Third, at your opponent's location you can ask for a plant tour. A significant amount of data can be gathered in this way. After a few hours in a plant you should be able to answer a lot of questions about it.

For example, if a seller comes to a buyer's office and says that his or her company's capacity for machining certain parts is *x* number of pieces per day, the buyer must accept the seller's statement unless he or she has been in the seller's plant and watched the machining process. Many pieces of information are used in a negotiation, and much of it comes from the operations of the plant. A plant visit is a must in order for you to verify the information your opponent uses.

Other advantages of negotiating at your opponent's location are: (1) It is much harder for someone in your organization to interrupt the negotiation, to ask you a question, to get some information, and so forth; (2) You can see others in your opponent's company who will not be in the actual negotiation. You may have the opportunity to acquire information from them; (3) You have the opportunity to get out of the office and get a change of scenery; and (4) You can use the tactic of having to check at your office before agreeing to something.

Another very important advantage is a psychological one. Most people believe that it is an advantage to negotiate at home. If your opponent believes this, then you gain the psychological edge if you suggest that the negotiation be held at your opponent's location. From your opponent's viewpoint, the only logical reason is that you must feel so confident of your position that you can "give away" the home-field advantage.

In discussing the advantage of conducting the negotiation in your location, several disadvantages to the opponent were noted. However, if you are the opponent negotiating in someone else's location, there are several ways you can offset these disadvantages. For example, you could arrive the day before the negotiation, take a long tour of the opponent's plant, and treat some of the production people who will not be participating in the negotiation to dinner. You can then update your plan based on the information you have gathered and thus be in a better position at the start of the negotiation. Another tactic, to offset the apparent disadvantage of having to leave at a certain time, is to make return transportation reservations for various times as well as, perhaps, a hotel reservation for the night.

## A Neutral Location

The major advantages of a neutral location are: (1) Neither side is likely to be interrupted. (If the location is a motel, you can tell the switchboard to hold all messages.) (2) Neither side has the advantage of being in its own, familiar location. (3) Since neither side can call on experts or get more data, they are starting even. (4) Both sides may have only a few negotiation team members, because of travel costs, problems, and so forth.

There are some ways you can gain an advantage in a neutral site. Handle all of the administration details. Arrive with a suitcase or a hanging bag with a change of clothes. Order all meals and snacks. And start the negotiation as follows: "I want to assure you that all of the details have been taken care of. First, at 10:15 coffee and rolls will be served in the room. Second, I've ordered soup and a variety of sandwiches for lunch. They will arrive about 12:30. Third, at 3:30 a coke and coffee break will be served. At that time, we will take orders for how everyone wants their dinner steaks cooked. Dinner will be served at 7:30. Besides the steak we'll have potatoes, vegetables, a mixed salad, and dessert. I checked and learned that the kitchen closes at 11:45, we can order a midnight snack about 11:30. So you don't have to worry. All the details have been arranged."

Your opponent will get the message that you are prepared to negotiate a very long time. This should give you a strong psychological advantage at the start of the negotiation.

I suggest that for each negotiation you review the three alternatives and pick the best for you.

The danger of becoming predictable were discussed earlier. Once you have become predictable and your opponent becomes aware of the pattern, you will have problems. So you should vary locations.

Where a negotiation is held is an important factor in determining the outcome of the negotiation. It is one that you cannot afford to overlook or to let your opponent decide.

Also, you should make other decisions related to the logistics of the negotiation.

## Timing

First, what time should the negotiation start? Are you a morning or afternoon person? Most people are more alert during certain parts of the day. If you are a morning person, it is best if you negotiate in the morning. It would not be very wise to start negotiations after lunch. You may not be able to always negotiate when you want, but you should be aware of this factor and, whenever possible, use it to your advantage.

Second, what day of the week is best? If you are negotiating at home this could be a big advantage. For example, if you start a negotiation at your plant Wednesday morning and at 5:00 P.M. no settlement is at hand, how much pressure is there on your opponent to leave? Not very much. Your opponent might have to reschedule a few appointments for Thursday and perhaps Friday, but that usually presents no conflict. But if you start a negotiation at your plant Friday morning and late in the afternoon no settlement is close, there is a lot of pressure on your opponent. It's often difficult to change reservations for Friday-night flights, leaving the prospect of waiting until Saturday and missing many personal plans. So, late Friday afternoon the opponent may give more than planned just to get a settlement that night and be able to make a flight home.

Third, when should you plan to stop? If you are negotiating at your opponent's plant, use the time to your advantage. For example, I have observed that many buyers are in car pools and must leave at closing time. In this situation, time pressure is on the buyer. The seller can wait patiently, not give in and win the negotiation.

An example of this concept (for buyers) is when I lived in Lima, Ohio, and there was one flight per day on Lake Central Airlines that went from Pittsburgh to Toledo, to Lima, and returned to Pittsburgh. When buyers were negotiating with sellers from Pittsburgh, if the sellers missed their plane, they had a 24 hour wait for the next flight. If it was Friday, the wait was until Monday since we didn't have week-end service. We, as buyers, tried to put a lot of time pressure on any Pittsburgh sales team that negotiated with us on any day, especially Friday.

## Related Administrative Details

### The Room

When negotiations are at home, you need to decide how the room will be set up. The shape of the table can be important. Round tables generally give a feeling of togetherness. It is not an us-them arrangement. If you are in a weak position, a round table may help you; it could be conducive to more friendly relations. Rectangular tables are us-them tables. Generally one team sits on one side and the other team on the other side. This is good if you are in a strong position. Be sure to have your team leader sit at the head of the table since this is the authority position at the table. (In our culture we tend to defer to the person at the head of the table.) This will underscore your strength and give a psychological boost to your position. If you have a "T" or "L" shape setup, be sure to sit at the end of the "L," the top of the "T."

There are other administrative details to be concerned with.

### Copies

Be sure to bring many extra sets of materials to pass out, charts, and so forth. It is possible that you will lose momentum or let your opponent "off the hook" if a negotiation session is stopped while extra copies are made of some piece of data.

### Visual Aids

Be sure you have all necessary chalkboards, flipcharts, and so forth. Again, delays could really hurt.

### Audiovisual Equipment

Be sure to check it before the negotiation. Have extra bulbs, take-up reels, and so forth. This may seem to be a small point, but it is important. If your opponent is in trouble and a bulb burns out and it takes you 15 minutes to get a new one, your opponent has time to regroup.

### Names and Titles

Be sure to get the names and titles of everyone on your opponent's side of the table. Keep these in front of you so you can call each person by name. Also, titles may help determine who has the power.

### Dirty Tricks

Finally, you should recognize "dirty tricks." Some people advocate that when you negotiate at your place you use dirty tricks such as placing the chairs of your opponents over a heat vent, or placing your opponents' chairs so that they face the window. That way they have light problems. Also, it will be easy for you to see the expression on their faces, but hard for them to see your expression. Another trick is to cut the front legs of the chairs your opponents will use a little shorter so they will keep sliding forward. A fourth is to put your opponents in very hard chairs. These kinds of tactics are juvenile and unprofessional and should not be used.

In summary, then, Checkpoint 21 covers all of the location and time decisions and miscellaneous administrative details. If these are not handled to your advantage, they could cost you during the negotiations.

## CHECKPOINT 22: ANALYZE SELF

During this checkpoint take a good look at yourself: the good and the bad. Your attitude, personality, behavior, strengths, and weaknesses will affect the negotiation.

What strengths do you have as a person that can help your side in the negotiations? Even more important, what weakness will hurt your side? A point to remember is that it is better to admit your weak points (and control them) than it is to have your opponent use your weak points.

For example, I tend to get upset when someone does not quickly grasp a very logical, step-by-step presentation. The longer it takes for another person to grasp the logic, the angrier I get. As I get angry, I could lose control of myself, I could lose control of the negotiation, and I could eventually lose the negotiation. In this area my behavior will really hurt my side of the negotiation table. So during this checkpoint I remind myself not to lose control.

The purpose of this checkpoint is to build on your positive points and to control your negative behaviors. What behaviors can hurt you? What behaviors can help you? Below are two lists. The first includes some negative behaviors. These must be controlled. The second includes a sample of positive behaviors. You must build on these and use them to your advantage. Any that apply to you should be marked and remembered before your next negotiation. You may add more to your individual list.

A.  Negative Behaviors

| | |
|---|---|
| Inconsistent | Arrogant |
| Uncreative | Data-bound |
| Impulsive | Stubborn |
| Impractical | Nit-picking |
| Manipulative | Distorts information/facts |

Perfectionist

Gambler

Domineering

Obligated to others

Reduces self-esteem

Passive

Easily influenced

Uses high pressure

Stingy

Avoids conflict

Too compromising

Says yes too often

Cannot prioritize information

Contentious

Plodding

Agitated

Gullible

Too committed to others

Discards ideas quickly

Too critical

Lacks convictions

Self-interested only

Impatient

Analyzes excessively

B.  Positive Behaviors

Seeks excellence

Helpful

Quick to act

Self-confident

Persuasive

Risk-taker

Persistent

Has sense of urgency

Practical

Economical

Factual

Steadfast

Detail-oriented

Analytical

Methodical

Adapts easily

Looks for new approaches

Resolves conflicts well

Flexible

Experimental

Tactful

Inspiring

Idealistic

Thoughtful

Receptive

Very responsive

Loyal

Cooperative

Leader

Looks for change

Competitive

Tenacious

Enthusiastic

Does what is best for

principal

Assures closure

Any others that apply to you must be added to your personal list. Before each negotiation, go over your list and remember to build on your strong points and control your weak points.

In summary, like the old song, this checkpoint states that each negotiator must accentuate your positives and eliminate (or control) your negatives, if the negotiation is to be successful.

## CHECKPOINT 23: BE PREPARED

On any normal day that the average amateur golfer plays his or her sport, what does the golfer usually do to prepare? Not very much! The normal procedure is to pick up the others in the foursome and drive to the golf course together. During the ride the conversation usually concerns business, family, spouses, or the latest jokes. Seldom does the discussion concern techniques for better golfing. Once at the course the golfers may change clothes, have a drink, and perhaps hit a dozen or so putts, then proceed to the first tee. Many times that first drive is terrible. Many times the first few holes are badly played. Often this leads to a badly played 18 holes of golf.

On any normal day that the average professional golfer plays golf, what does he or she usually do to prepare? Many things! The standard procedure is to hit 200–300 practice balls. (Often the professional will stay after the game and hit more practice balls.) The professional will also practice putting for a long time. When the pro hits the first drive it is usually great. And usually all of the 18 holes are played well.

On the first tee the amateur golfer is not ready to play. On the first tee the professional golfer is ready to play golf. The analogy holds for negotiations. The negotiations professional prepares to negotiate. When the negotiation starts, the professional is ready; the amateur is not.

For example, on the day of a normal negotiations, the average buyer may do the following types of things before the negotiation starts: send out quotes for other items; approve invoices; expedite materials; check receipts; place orders; attend meetings; work on cost reductions; answer questions; request information for engineering; process paperwork; review computer reports. Before the buyer realizes it, he or she gets a call from the reception desk saying that XYZ Company is on the premises (to negotiate). The buyer says, "Send them in," looks for the appropriate files, and before the buyer knows it, the negotiation has started. At this point (the first tee), the buyer is not at all prepared to negotiate.

Many times the sales team also is not prepared. They may have to travel to the buyer's city. They may rise early, rush to the airport, stand in line to check in, wait for the proper time to board the plane, endure the hassle of crowded planes, land and wait for people to get off, wait for luggage, wait in line to rent a car, drive to the buyer's office, sign in, and finally walk to the buyer's office. At this point, the sales team is not prepared to negotiate.

There are many examples of this same phenomenon in other types of negotiations. Almost all of the time one side is more prepared to negotiate than the other side. The side that is most prepared will start the negotiation in a stronger position. Assuming everything else in the negotiation is equal, this position of initial strength will continue throughout the negotiation.

The professional negotiator understands this and prepares. In some ways a negotiation is similar to being on stage or participating in an athletic contest. The adrenaline should be flowing. All senses should be alert.

Each negotiator should start preparing from the time of getting out of bed on the morning of a negotiation (especially a major negotiation). Think about the negotiation, and think positively about your participation in it. Look your best! Think your best!

One warning about how to dress. Do not wear the same outfit every time you negotiate or are ready to consummate a deal. Think of one buyer I know of who had a special suit. Whenever the buyer was ready to place an order, he wore his best pin-striped suit. The seller knew that if the buyer had the special suit on, he was going to get an order that day or that someone would get an order, but that if the buyer was not wearing the suit, the negotiations that day would not lead to an order. On the latter days, the observant seller would not give on important issues because he had nothing to gain.

The important point is that to be successful in negotiations you must prepare yourself on the day of the negotiation. If the negotiation will last for a few days or many weeks, remember that each day is important and deserves the same preparation.

## CHECKPOINT 24: DOCUMENT RESULTS

Column 15 of the MAP (Figure 4-21) should be used to list the final outcome of each issue negotiated. Column 16 should be used to show the delta ($+$ or $-$) in comparison with your objective (Figure 4-22).

Strong Position

A. M. Boss  
Signature

| ① Issues | ② Type | ③ $V_M$ | ④ $V_{MR}$ | ⑤ $V_{OR}$ | ⑥ $V_O$ | ⑦ Authority Limit | ⑧ Information | ⑨ Agenda | ⑩ $IP_M$ | ⑪ $O_M$ | ⑫ $O_O$ | ⑬ $IP_O$ | ⑭ Tactics | ⑮ Results | ⑯ |
|---|---|---|---|---|---|---|---|---|---|---|---|---|---|---|---|
| Cash Terms | W | 1% = $2,700 | | | 1% = $2,700 | Net 30 days | 2 | 3 | 3% in 30 days | 2% in 15 days | 1% in 10 days | Net in 30 days | Lower than the boss | | |
| | | | | | | | | | | | | | | | |
| | | | | | | | | | | | | | | | |
| | | | | | | | | | | | | | | | |
| Avoid Issues | | | | | | | | | | | | | | | |
| Lead Time | — | $5,000/week | | | $10,000/week | Max 13 weeks | 7 | — | — | — | 13 weeks | 27 weeks | — | | |

FIGURE 4-21  MAP

| ① | ② | ③ | ④ | ⑤ | ⑥ | ⑦ | ⑧ | ⑨ | ⑩ | ⑪ | ⑫ | ⑬ | ⑭ | ⑮ | ⑯ |
|---|---|---|---|---|---|---|---|---|---|---|---|---|---|---|---|
| Issues | Type | $V_m$ | $V_{MR}$ | $V_{OR}$ | $V_o$ | Authority Limit | Information | Agenda | $IP_m$ | $O_m$ | $O_o$ | $IP_o$ | Tactics | Results | Delta |
| Cash Terms | W | 1% = $2,700 | | | 1% = $2,700 | Net 30 days | 2 | 3 | 3% in 30 days | 2% in 15 days | 1% in 10 days | Net in 30 days | Lower than the boss | | |
| | | | | | | | | | | | | | | | |
| | | | | | | | | | | | | | | | |
| | | | | | | | | | | | | | | | |
| Avoid Issues Lead Time | — | $5,000/ week | | | $10,000/ week | Max 13 weeks | 7 | — | — | — | 13 weeks | 27 weeks | — | | |

**FIGURE 4-22** MAP

The summation of Column 15 is the overall result of your efforts, your report card for the negotiation. It is important to remember that the objectives should be very challenging. (Refer to Checkpoint 17.) If you meet every objective in any negotiation your objectives were too low, or your opponent was very weak. Column 15 must be considered in this light. It must be evaluated in a relative way as compared to objectives and an absolute way as compared to total dollars "won."

A purchasing manager once asked, "What would you do for a buyer who met every one of the objectives in a negotiation?" The real question was aimed at giving buyers a bonus, just as many sellers get a bonus for exceeding a sales objective. I answered that if a buyer worked for me and exceeded every objective in every negotiation I would fire the buyer. When asked why, I reviewed the negotiations diagram (see Chapter 2). I tried to convince him that really challenging objectives would gain his company better actual results, even if buyers did not meet all of the objectives.

Many people feel frustrated when they participate in negotiations. They wonder how they can prove to their bosses that they did a good job negotiating. Buyers, sellers, management, labor, and other negotiators must report to a boss, and many times to their principal. All of them feel this frustration. This can be especially true if the boss has never participated in the negotiation process as a lead negotiator. It is almost always true if the boss has never been in the negotiation arena.

Columns 15 and 16 are part of the planning process on our form. Although they will be used after the negotiation, they must be included when the MAP form is set up. They can help significantly in showing your boss what was accomplished.

## CHECKPOINT 25: PREPARE TO LISTEN

One of the most important concessions you can give to your opponent is to listen. This is especially true if your opponent is making a proposal. Most of us want to talk too much, especially at the negotiating table. I know of one negotiator who put an "L" in the middle of the face of his watch. "L" stood for listen. Every time he looked at his watch he was reminded to listen.

I have seen a purchasing team in a mock negotiation lose the opportunity to get the best agreement ever negotiated because they could not stop talking. The buyers had been told they were not allowed to buy at more than $92,311. The sellers had been told that because of antitrust problems they could not sell below $99,109. The sellers had also been told that the profit on the item was $35,227 after *all* costs.

At a first glance, it appears as if the case can never be solved. It is impossible to reach agreement if the buyer cannot buy above $92,311 and the seller cannot sell below $99,109. But the key is creative selling. Can a seller structure an offer to be legal and within the buyer's limit? The seller has a lot of room to move with $35,227 of pure profit. The successful sellers are the ones that offer research and development (R&D) contracts, strategic studies contracts, and so forth that pay the buyer at least $7,000. During a caucus the sales team prepared a proposal to offer a $15,000 R&D contract and a price of $99,109. They were sure that they would get an order and *still* make approximately $20,000 profit, which was slightly more than 20 percent.

When negotiations resumed, the sellers, since they had asked for the caucus, spoke first. The sales manager said, "Here is our offer. First, the price will be $99,109. . . ." At that point the purchasing manager pounded his fist on the table and yelled, "I told you we would not pay $99,109 for your product. If that's the best you can do, get out. This negotiation is over." If that person had waited about 10 seconds longer, he would have heard the sales manager continue, "We want to offer a research and development contract in which we will pay your company $15,000 to give us an evaluation of our product in your application." The sales manager was then prepared to show how the net effect for the buyer was a purchase price of $84,109 plus the minimum cost of preparing the information that the purchasing manager's company already had.

Had the purchasing manager listened, he would have been able to make the best net purchase that I have ever seen offered in this case study. One of the most important behaviors in negotiations is to listen. Also remember that if you listen, people will generally like you and you might even learn something.

When the other side is ready to make a proposal, you should not only listen to it completely but also write down the salient points of it. This is *not* a sign of weakness. It is an inexpensive concession that you stand to gain from. After the proposal is made, read it back to assure that you understand it completely.

If you cannot agree at this point, all you have to do is say "no." If a few parts are acceptable, these might form the foundation of a counterproposal. But you have lost nothing by listening.

You should keep all the notes containing your opponent's proposals. These will provide a good history of the negotiation. You might also take the best parts of many proposals and put together a new proposal which includes only your opponent's previous offers. (How can your opponent say no?)

Remember the expression "Your mind and your mouth cannot be open at the same time." Listening is a key to winning the negotiation. During the planning of any negotiation you should remind yourself to listen in the actual negotiation.

Now that we have reviewed the 25 point checklist, the next tool to discuss is consideration of all of the issues to be negotiated. Chapters 5, 6, 7, 8, and 9 review the issues in specific types of negotiations.

# CHAPTER 5

# Buyer-Seller Issues to be Negotiated

The issues discussed in this chapter are not listed in order of importance. The importance will be different in each negotiation you conduct. The professional negotiator does not have an overall priority ranking of the issues to be negotiated. The negotiator objectively looks at them in relationship to the particular negotiation to be conducted.

The issues below have been grouped in logical families for ease in reading. Each issue must be given equal consideration, especially in the planning phase of a negotiation. The purpose of this list is to assure that you do not forget any issue during the planning stage of a negotiation.

## PRICE

This is always the first issue any buyer or seller thinks of when asked for a list of issues to be negotiated. For that reason only, the list begins with price. Remember it is possible to win the price part of a negotiation and lose the total negotiation.

Several factors concerning price should be considered. First, what is a fair price? For years, many people have tried to develop a definition of fair price that is acceptable to everyone. But it is impossible to define the term "fair price" or "reasonable price" because what is fair or reasonable to one side of the negotiating table may be very unfair to the other side.

During 1974–1975, many car owners did not believe that a price of $.67 per gallon for gasoline was fair. They certainly did not believe it was reasonable, and they were most unhappy with the price. At the same time, gas station owners were saying the price was still too low. In 1980, gasoline cost $1.27 per gallon. The car owners were unhappy. They would have paid $1.00 per gallon without question. As a matter of fact, the car owners would have been very happy to pay "only" $1.00 even though a few years earlier they were unhappy with $.67. The point is that you cannot define fair and/or reasonable price. The accurate reference is to state it is an "acceptable" price, one at which the buyer will buy and the seller will sell. The only way to quantify price is to say it is acceptable.

Many times buyers have paid prices that were so high that they were not fair, reasonable, or justifiable, or, in many cases, legal, ethical, or moral. However, the buyers really needed the product so that price was acceptable. Many times a seller has sold at very low prices to maintain a cash flow for the seller's company. The seller needed the order very badly, so the price was acceptable, even if it meant a negative profit.

Another factor in the price issue is the quote. A quote is defined three ways:

1.  It is a price level at which a seller would like to do business. The seller should make substantial profit at the quoted level, under normal conditions.

**2.** It is the starting point for most industrial negotiations.

**3.** It is a number the seller feels can be supported at the start of the negotiation.

A quote can be and usually is changed before the buyer places an order. The important thing to remember is that a quote is not a "concrete" number.

A third factor affecting price considerations is that a low price does not always equal low value. Sometimes high price means low value. Consider this item from the December 22, 1977, *Wall Street Journal.*

> *The more expensive a product, the better quality it must be. Right? Wrong. A study by Peter C. Riesz, an associate professor of marketing at the University of Iowa, affirms what many consumers have long suspected—that high price and high quality do not necessarily go hand-in-hand. In fact, says Mr. Riesz, it often happens that the brand with the highest price tag is, in fact, the lowest quality. This is especially true for such items as soap, cosmetics, toilet articles, and convenience foods. Suntan lotions, frozen pizzas, and childrens' clothing show the highest negative correlation between price and quality.\**

Companies and marketing specialists are well aware of consumer reliance on price as a guide to quality and sometimes price their goods accordingly," adds the professor. He tells of a new mustard that was packaged in a crockery jar. It flopped when the processor tried to sell it for 49 cents, but turned into a gold mine when the price was changed to 81 cents a jar.

Many times buyers make the mistake of believing that a low-priced item is of low quality. This attitude has cost the United States many jobs. After the Second World War, everything made in Japan was cheap and of very low quality. This changed, however, and by the late 1950s, the quality was improving, but the prices were still low. Consumers tried the low-priced goods and found that the quality was equal to (sometimes better) than U.S.-made products. Many American manufacturers did not believe the goods made in Japan were valid competition, so they did not react. By the time these manufacturers reacted, it was too late.

Every buyer has the obligation to check out lower-priced items to determine whether the quality is equal to the higher-priced supplier's quality. Many bargains are available.

Sellers must be aware of this factor and try to use it to their advantage. This is especially true if the seller is able to quote lower than average market level prices.

A fourth factor in considering price is that a price should reinforce the buyer's perception of the value of the product or service to the buyer. Sellers should always start their decision-making process by identifying potential customers and their needs. Needs analysis is a most important part of any pricing policy. The more the perceived need, the greater the desire, the higher the price the seller can ask, and the more profit the seller's company can make.

A fifth consideration is that cost plays a subordinate role in pricing. It is really a final check or guideline for the minimum acceptable price. The seller should get as much as possible for each product he sells. Many concepts from economics are important, including (1) the demand curve, (2) price elasticity, and (3) the point where marginal revenue equals marginal cost and contribution is maximized.

Finally, the concept of uniqueness must be considered by both buyers and sellers. If the seller's product has something very unique (that no one else has), the seller is in the power position. The buyer must do everything possible to downplay distinctive uniqueness and must never admit that he or she needs the unique part of the seller's product.

An example is the Ford Motor Company's three-way tailgate on their station wagons. A few years ago Ford was the only company that had a three-way tailgate and a large part of its advertising budget was spent on this feature of the car. If Ford could convince a potential station wagon buyer that the buyer "had to have" a three-way tailgate, Ford had a confirmed customer.

## QUANTITY DISCOUNTS

Many items are sold using a volume/price schedule. Nuts and bolts are a good example. A typical price schedule for one of these items might look like this.

1,000 items at 90 cents each
5,000 items at 72 cents each
10,000 items at 57 cents each
20,000 items at 50 cents each
50,000 items at 42 cents each
100,000 items at 35 cents each
250,000 items at 27 cents each

Buyers might want to negotiate the next-higher quantity level, suggesting that their quantity needs will probably rise. This tactic is known as the "bracket bounce." Buyers should always try to get prices for volumes that are higher than they will actually buy.

Many items do not usually have a volume/price schedule. This does not mean that the buyer should not negotiate for such a schedule. In fact, since the seller may not be prepared at all to negotiate such a schedule, the buyer may come out ahead on this issue (or be given another issue instead).

## DOWN PAYMENTS

Today, the cost of money is very, very high. The seller's company will have to invest money in materials, labor, and so forth to manufacture a product for the buyer. The seller can make a very logical argument as to why the buyer must provide a down payment with the purchase order. This issue will probably come up in many negotiations.

## PROGRAM PAYMENTS/PROGRESS PAYMENTS/ PROGRESSIVE PAYMENTS/PASS THROUGH PAYMENTS

These terms may seem very similar, but there are major differences. All relate to payments during the life of a contract.

Progress payments are payments made by a buyer to the seller based upon something actually being accomplished. When the seller completes 10 percent of the work (building a new plant for example), the buyer will pay the seller 10 percent of the total contract. In many cases, the buyer will keep one percent as a retainage (see Retainage subheading below).

Another example would be a buyer paying the seller for the cost of the materials the seller purchases to complete the buyer's order. Some evidence (a packing list, for example) is generally required before the buyer will send a check. The important point is that payment is only made based upon progress being accomplished toward completion of the buyer's order.

Program and progressive payments are based upon a negotiated schedule which has nothing to do with completion of work. An example of a program payment would be:

10% with the purchase order

20% three months after date of purchase order

40% seven months after date of purchase order

20% nine months after date of purchase order

10% collect upon delivery

An example of progressive payments is a 5 percent-per-month schedule.

Pass through payments are when one company pays its suppliers on the same basis as its customer's pay it. So whenever the company receives a payment toward an open contract, it will pay its suppliers their "share" of the total.

There are significant advantages and disadvantages to all four methods of payment. From the buyer's viewpoint, progress payments and pass through payments are the only two acceptable plans. Buyers can be hurt by progressive payments. For example, a general contractor who agreed to "help" a small subcontractor paid 7 percent per month for a job that should have taken 13 months to complete. The general manager was very busy and his site manager somewhat lazy. When nine payments had been made, only 17 percent of the actual work had been completed. The subcontractor announced that he was broke, could not complete the job, and was filing for bankruptcy. (Of course, his house, car, etc. were in his wife's name.) The general contractor now had to find another subcontractor but was in a very poor negotiating position and had to agree to a time-and-material contract. The cost to complete and remaining 83 percent of the work turned out to be 97 percent of the original contract. In total, the general contractor paid checks totaling 160 percent of the original contract to get 100 percent of the work accomplished. He made a major mistake when he agreed to progressive payments.

From the seller's viewpoint, the more money the seller can receive upfront, the better. If the seller has the money before making final delivery, he or she does not have to worry about hiring bill collectors and can reduce the number of accounts receivable and treasury employees. The professional poker player, and most active amateurs, have the philosophy that it is best to play poker with the other player's money. So, the professional works very hard at winning the early pots. The less money the others have, the more they can be squeezed on close hands later in the game.

## FIRM PRICE/PRICE PROTECTION/PRICE AT TIME OF SHIPMENT/PRICE AT TIME OF ORDER

In today's environment, the goal of every buyer should be to get a firm price for every purchase order the buyer places. Many companies have gone out of business because the prices they paid for raw materials, purchased parts, and other goods and services went up much faster than the prices they received for their products. It is very difficult to conduct business if you do not know the cost of your purchased materials until after the materials are received. How can a business make plans in this type of environment? It is very hard, if costs cannot be controlled or forecast.

The seller, of course, should resist firm prices. The seller can make a logical argument that the seller should be allowed to price the products *after* all costs have been actually determined. That way neither the buyer nor the seller is taking a risk.

## PRICE ESCALATION/ESCALATION INDEX/ ESCALATION STARTING DATE/ESCALATION BASE/ ESCALATION RATIO

More and more, we see these five issues included in negotiations for all sizes of industrial and commercial orders. The first item to be considered is whether there will be any escalation clause in the contract at all. This is a major point today, and if the buyer agrees to an escalation clause in the contract, the buyer should receive something major in return. It is not true that all sellers are entitled to price escalation. The seller should prepare a logical, rational presentation, rather than an emotional pitch if the seller wants to win the price escalation point. Once the buyer and seller have agreed to include an escalation clause, the escalation negotiation has really only just begun. The index that will be used, the starting date, the basepoint, and the ratio must be discussed. This is one area in which a negotiator must really do his or her homework.

There are hundreds of different indexes published by the government and private sources. Ideally, an index should behave exactly like the product being negotiated. The trick is to find an index that behaves like the product. All the error, of course, should be in your favor.

The starting date is most important. The seller should expect that escalation starts with the date of the order. In some cases, the seller does not do anything for several months. A wise buyer should take the position that escalation should not start to affect the order until the seller starts to buy material, employ labor, or commit other resources toward it.

The basepoint is the date which will be used to pick a number on the index to compare to a later point. The basepoint date and starting date do *not* have to be the same. Both are negotiable.

For example, it is possible to place a purchase order on October 9th, have the basepoint be October 1st, and have the escalation starting date be November 20th. The ratio is relationship between movement of the index and movement of the contract price. For example, if the index moves one percent, the price on the purchase order will change by $13.

## ESCALATION STOP DATE

This is a very important point for buyers. If an order is late, buyers should take the position that they will not pay any escalation after the due date. The seller is at fault when the seller ships late. Buyers are paying a large penalty because of late delivery. Why should they pay

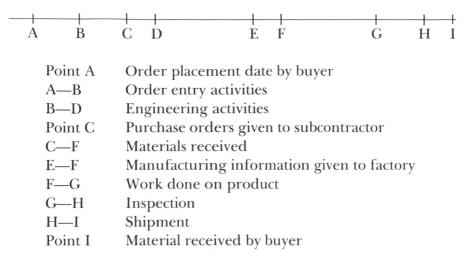

| | |
|---|---|
| Point A | Order placement date by buyer |
| A—B | Order entry activities |
| B—D | Engineering activities |
| Point C | Purchase orders given to subcontractor |
| C—F | Materials received |
| E—F | Manufacturing information given to factory |
| F—G | Work done on product |
| G—H | Inspection |
| H—I | Shipment |
| Point I | Material received by buyer |

**Figure 5-1**    Major activities during a major contract

a double penalty? If buyers negotiate an escalation stop date, they may win twice. First, no extra payments will be made and, second, the vendor will have extra incentive to complete the order on time.

During the time of the highest inflation in the United States, a supplier could make several thousands of dollars by shipping one week late. Consider a contract ship date of March 23rd. By waiting until April 1, when the index used to measure inflation would show a significant increase, the supplier could get a higher price.

Figure 5-1 illustrates a concept that buyers should be very aware of and use during escalation negotiation. It shows major activities during a major contract. (These activities are discussed under the Lead Time subheading below.)

The only impact of inflation on material costs for this contract is during the time from C—F. After point F, no matter what happens to inflation it cannot affect this contract because all of the material has been received. Buyers should negotiate escalation start and stop dates for each part of the contract. Sellers, on the other hand, should negotiate for the A—I period.

## MATERIAL PRICE PROTECTION

When a buyer makes a firm commitment to a seller, the seller should be in a position to make firm commitments to his or her suppliers.

This should mean that within a couple of weeks, the seller's material costs should be fixed. Once these costs have been established, a major percentage of the seller's total costs are locked in. A wise buyer will negotiate this point and ask for price protection for the total material percentage in his or her product. The seller does not lose anything and the buyer protects himself or herself.

## MANUFACTURING PRICE BREAKS

This point is aimed at the seller's manufacturing process. Each and every process has certain logical break points. In the steel industry, a logical break would be one heat of steel. During the negotiations process, a buyer should, if at all possible, negotiate quantities that equal manufacturing price breaks. Because there is no excess scrap and because the manufacturer is utilizing 100 percent of one manufacturing lot, the buyer should expect lower prices.

## HOW LONG IS THE QUOTE VALID?

The seller should always put a limit on the length of time the quote is valid. This now may become an issue in the negotiation and this, also, puts time pressure on the buyer. The seller can agree to a 60-day period, rather than 30-day period, but the seller should ask for something in return. This simple tactic will, in most circumstances, gain a smaller issue for the sales side. Both sides should always prepare for this negotiation issue.

## CONSIGNED STOCKING/LOCAL STOCKING/ DISTRIBUTOR STOCKING/SUPPLIER STOCKING/IN- PROCESS STOCKING/RAW MATERIAL STOCKING

From the buyer's viewpoint, the more inventory the supplier carries, the less inventory the buyer must carry. The cost of carrying inventory is very high. The usual estimates range from 20–33 percent per year to carry inventory. This includes the cost of money, the cost of space, the cost of moving inventory, the cost of controlling inventory, and so forth. The buyer's objective should be to transfer as much of this cost as possible to his or her vendors.

From the buyer's side, the best possible of all stocking arrangements is "consigned stock." This is an agreement whereby the seller puts inventory into the buyer's location, but retains title to the material. Since the title is still with the seller, the material does not show up in the buyer's inventory. Thus, the buyer's assets are reduced, and his or her return on investment is higher. At the same time, since the material is at the buyer's location, the buyer can use it any time the material is needed. The buyer has the best of both worlds: material on hand to use whenever a requirement is generated and low dollars invested in inventory. It is normal in most industrial situations for the buyer to guarantee to the seller that once material is delivered to the buyer's plant, the buyer will eventually pay for it.

The buyer cannot expect the seller to assume the risk of obsolescence, as well as the cost of carrying inventory.

The next best deal from the buyer's side is "local stocking." This is a situation whereby the seller stocks material in the seller's warehouse in the buyer's town. The material is very close to the buyer, but since it is on the seller's property, the seller has more control over the material. If the buyer does not have room to store material, this may be the most attractive deal. The only problem is transportation when the buyer needs it. For example, a local truck strike would stop all deliveries. Even though the material is only five miles away, it would be of no use to the buyer. Another problem would be cost. If the seller does not normally have need of a warehouse in the buyer's town, establishing a warehouse would increase the seller's cost.

"Distributor stocking" may be similar to local stocking in that the distributor may be in the buyer's city. The distributor may be several miles away. In this situation transportation could be a problem. Another major problem for the buyer could happen if the distributor sold the material to someone else. This could easily happen if an "emergency" condition existed. A buyer must be careful of distributor stocking. Sellers should have this as their first objective if they are agreeable to stocking in or near to the buyer's city.

"Supplier stocking" means that the seller stocks completed material, ready for shipment, at his or her plant. The buyer can call up the vendor first thing in the morning and usually the seller can ship that day. The seller has complete control of all of his or her material. The seller could use this material for emergency shipment to other customers, assuming of course the specifications are common. The buyer can usually be assured of same-day shipment and generally next-day delivery. The possible problems with this arrangement are transportation strikes and weather. No seller in his or her right mind would guarantee delivery from Buffalo during the winter because of that city's history of snowfall. Again, the material in stock is of no use to the buyer, if Buffalo is snowed in.

Manufacturing people in general, and first-line manufacturing supervisors in particular, like to "lay on hands." That is, they like to touch inventory. Material shortages are the most typical reason that manufacturing people fall short of meeting their production commitments. Manufacturing supervisors get into the most trouble when they "miss the load." Buyers can make important positive points with their manufacturing people if they negotiate deals which assure purchased material is always available when the manufacturing people need the material.

If the buyer cannot get the seller to agree to stock finished parts (either in the buyer's plant, a local site, or the seller's plant), the next best deal is "in-process stocking." This is an agreement whereby the seller stocks semifinished products.

For example, if the buyer is buying cold-rolled sheet steel, the buyer might negotiate a deal for the seller to stock hot bands. When the buyer needs material, all the seller has to do is take the hot bands out of stock, process them on the cold mill, and ship the finished product to the buyer. Another example is aluminum die castings that are machined to different configurations. In this example, the seller would agree to stock so many raw castings. Whenever the buyer has a requirement, the seller will take these raw castings out of stock, complete the necessary machining operations, and ship the finished parts to the buyer.

The last type of agreement, "raw material stocking," is one whereby the seller agrees to inventory a certain quantity of raw materials. This significantly reduces the seller's lead time and enables production of the buyer's order to begin the day the seller receives the order.

All of these different stocking programs have the purpose of reducing the amount of inventory the buyer must carry to assure continued production in the buyer's plant.

## CONSIGNED STOCK TAX/CONSIGNED STOCK AUDITS/CONSIGNED STOCK INSURANCE COSTS

If a buyer and seller agree that they will do business on a consigned stock basis, three more issues must be negotiated. In many states, there are taxes on inventory and/or taxes on property. Who will pay these taxes? Both sides can make a very logical presentation. The buyer can argue that since the seller still has title to the material, the seller should pay all applicable taxes. The seller can counter with the argument that it is the buyer's material, on the buyer's property, for the buyer's exclusive use, and that since the buyer will derive the major benefit from the stocking of the material, he or she should pay the taxes. Both sides can expand upon these arguments and negotiating this issue can take a long time.

Most auditors will require an actual count at least once a year for inventory stored at a customer's location. This is standard procedure. Most prudent businesspeople will require insurance coverage for this inventory. Who will pay these costs? These issues are very negotiable.

## LEAD TIME

If the buyer is not successful in negotiating an acceptable stocking agreement, lead time will probably become a major concern. The longer the lead time, the more inventory the buyer's company must carry. With a stocking program, this point should be covered since neither side wants to see an excessive amount of material stocked, because of the costs involved. There are numerous factors that contribute to lead time which might be negotiable points.

### Order Processing Time

This is the time from which a buyer's company produces an order until it gets into the seller's system. The mail room, a few secretaries, possibly a couple of computers, and a customer service clerk are generally involved in this stage. Many companies will also have a step in which the order is "priced out." Several steps generally are required before an order is really an order.

### Engineering Wait Time

Most items will require some type of engineering action. This will range from a complete new design that may take weeks or months to finish, to a quick review and "sign off." Since the seller cannot afford to pay engineers to just sit and wait for orders to arrive, any particular order must go into the queue. Engineering wait time is usually a significant part of total lead time.

### Engineering Time

This is the actual time any order is being worked on by the seller's engineers.

### Drafting Wait Time/Drafting Time

After the engineering section has completed its work, the information must be put into drawings and specifications. Again, each order will be faced with the time for waiting its turn before any action is taken on that order.

### Manufacturing Information Time

This step in the process determines how the product will be produced: What materials must be purchased from outside and what items will be manufactured inside. Detailed instructions must be written for the manufacturing department. This step generally also includes scheduling for future production. The normal functions involved in this step are manufacturing engineering, production control, inventory control, scheduling, manufacturing information methods, and industrial engineering.

## Purchasing Time

This step in the process involves two points. The purchasing department must first determine who to buy from and then place the order. And second, that supplier's lead time must be considered.

## Receiving, Inspection, and Storage Time

This step in the process is often overlooked. It could take up to a week to accomplish these three steps, for purchased material.

## Manufacturing Wait Time

One of the major objectives of the manufacturing function is to "make the load." Each plant manager, each general supervisor has an objective to "make the load" every day. This person must make a certain number of items or accomplish a certain amount of work. The manufacturing game is a numbers' game. The most important indicator of performance is productivity. This is simply a ratio of two numbers: net allowed hours divided by total hours.

For every item produced, a certain number of direct labor hours are required. These are standard hours or allowed hours. For example, if you were manufacturing felt tip pens, one labor step might be to place the cap on the body. The standard for this might be five seconds. For every pen produced, the supervisor would be allowed five seconds. At the end of each day, the total number of pens produced would be multiplied by five seconds to get the total net allowed hours. If one person put on 5,000 caps per day, that person's section would be allowed 6.9 hours of work ($5{,}000 \div 12 = 416$ minutes $\div 60 = 6.9$ hours). The productivity for that day would be $6.9 \div 8.0$. The more work the supervisor can get produced, the higher is his or her productivity.

The point of this is that a smart supervisor will have many jobs ready for each of the machines in his or her section. See Figure 5-2 for an example. This figure represents a small section with four machines. Each job must go on each of the machines. The supervisor

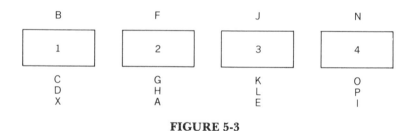

**FIGURE 5-2**  Job wait time

will have job A running on machine 1, with at least three jobs waiting (B, C, D). When job A is finished, the worker can have no excuses for being idle. When job A is finished and moves on to machine 2, it goes to the end of the line. This will be true for each machine. See Figure 5-3 that shows the position after all four jobs (A, E, I, M) have been completed. Job M is now shipped and job X is the new one.

**FIGURE 5-3**

## Manufacturing Move Time

This is the time necessary to move the material from machine 1 to machine 2.

## Actual Manufacturing Time

This is the actual time spent working on the product. This should be very close to the net allowed or standard time for each product. When people talk about manufacturing time, they generally mean the actual manufacturing time. For many products, the move time and the wait time are significant and could be greater than the actual work time. When buyers ask about how long it takes to make a product, the answer that they get is generally the actual manufacturing time, or the allowed time. Buyers, be careful.

It is a fact in many manufacturing plants that the move time and the wait time is significantly greater than the actual manufacturing time.

## Inspection, Packing, and Shipping Time

These three steps can also take up to a week. Negotiations do not get as deeply involved in lead time as they should. As has been described, there are many components of lead time. Most will affect every order. Of course, there are differences between job shop operations and assembly line operations. But lead time must be considered based upon its components. It should not be just briefly reviewed.

## DELIVERY DATE

For one-shot purchase orders, a firm date must be negotiated.

## PENALTY CLAUSE/CONSEQUENTIAL DAMAGES/ LIQUIDATED DAMAGES

To attempt to insure that the buyer receives the material on the delivery date, the buyer has at least three different points to negotiate whose purpose is to penalize the seller for late delivery.

A penalty clause is just that. If the supplier ships late, the supplier is charged so many dollars per day, per week, or per month. There is no attempt made to justify the charge. In general, it is just an arbitrary number that is agreed to by the buyer and seller. It is an incentive to the seller to ship on time since the seller will lose money if the seller is late. (It is like telling children that if they are late for supper, they cannot watch television. There is no direct relationship between the action and the penalty.) You must be careful with this point. In some states a one-way penalty clause is against the law. In these states, if the buyer asks for a penalty for late delivery, the buyer must be willing to offer an incentive for early delivery.

Consequential damages as I will define them are costs that result because of the failure of a supplier's part. These generally include all costs. For example, if the magnet wire failed in a small motor in a washing machine and a fire started that completely burned down a house, the owner could sue the magnet wire supplier for the total costs to build and furnish a new house. A smart buyer will get all of the buyer's suppliers to share in any liability the buyer's company may have in this area.

Liquidated damages, again as I define them are the agreed-upon direct costs that result because of the failure of a supplier's part or late delivery. For example, if a machine is supposed to be delivered on March 11 and will require an unloading crew and unloading equipment, the buyer and seller could agree ahead of time that the supplier will pay $X$ dollars per day to cover the costs of paying the crew and renting the equipment from March 11 until the machine is actually delivered and unloaded.

These three points have become more and more important today and should be included in most major negotiations.

## TOOLING

Many items require some type of tooling to produce the part. Examples would be a die mold for a die-cast part; a die for a stamped part, a special jig or fixture for a machine part, and so forth. "Tooling" will be used to cover all of the various items that could be involved. This will cover many more items than you may realize. Sellers in particular should try to get their customers to pay all the costs of tooling. Sellers should talk to their manufacturing people to determine if *anything* is special in the way of tools, fixtures, jigs, and so forth and, if so, negotiate the cost.

When there is tooling involved many related factors must be negotiated. These are discussed under the 15 subheadings that follow.

### Design

Who will design the tool is the first consideration. If the buyer's people design the tool, they will have the complete responsibility for the quality of the parts produced. They will have complete authority to make the design any way they want it to be, but they must also accept the responsibility.

If the buyer's people design the tool, the buyer should ask for a deduction in the tool cost. The seller's standard pricing formula will have a percentage for design time. This cost should not be incurred if the buyer's engineers design the tool.

The buyer will have a strong point here. If the seller designs the tool the seller must take complete responsibility for the quality of the final parts. When considering this point, a buyer must weigh the advantage of saving money (if the buyer's people design the tool) versus the advantage of having 100 percent of the responsibility placed on the supplier (if the seller designs the tool).

### Flexibility

The design must be flexible so as to be able to manufacture many parts or subparts.

### Payment

Who will pay the cost to produce the tool and whether this a partial payment or a complete payment is also most important. Many sellers charge only a part of the total cost so that in the future the buyer does not have the ability to remove the tools and give them to another supplier. The seller may just quote a "tool charge" or a "tool cost." The buyer must be sure to understand whether this covers all costs or just some of the costs. Many a buyer has told a supplier (after problems, a price increase, or as a strategy) to pack up the tools and ship them to the buyer's plant only to have the supplier respond that the buyer only paid part of the original cost and must pay $X$ dollars more if he or she wants the tool. These buyers were in a bad position.

The buyer must also understand what all goes into the tool charge. If the seller is making the tool in the seller's plant, what rates are being used? Are materials charged at cost or with an adder? Is overhead included? Actually, the buyer may have to do a cost analysis just on the tooling. These points certainly are important and allow for much negotiating room.

## Ownership

Who owns the tool also must be decided. The title can only be in one party (seller or buyer). This point is most important when negotiating payment, rental, maintenance, replacement costs, and use of the tool.

## Maintenance

All tools need maintenance. For example, a die-cast die should be cleaned and polished, and a stamping die needs to be sharpened. Who pays these costs? Both sides can take logical positions to defend themselves from paying for maintenance. The buyer can state that the die is the complete responsibility of the seller, so the seller should pay, or that the seller's employees may not take good care of the tool, so the seller should pay. How can I, the buyer asks, be expected to pay for maintenance when I cannot control the workers? The seller can state that maintenance is directly related to amount produced and the buyer controls quantity, so the buyer should pay.

## Replacement Costs

All tools wear out and must be replaced. Who pays these costs? As with the maintenance issue, both sides can present strong cases that the opponent should pay. Again, the point to remember is that this item should be negotiated. It may be easy to win because tool replacement is generally a few years into the future. Many negotiators (especially amateurs) have very short visions. They want to win something today or something that pays off today. They may be willing to give up (i.e., agree to pay) replacement costs. (They may even say to themselves, "I will not be here when the tool is replaced, so why worry about it.") With a high rate of inflation, replacement costs may be double the original cost.

Another important point to remember is that the total tool may not need to be replaced. For example, for a stamping die, the die shoe may last much longer than the die itself. If a buyer agrees to pay the replacement costs, the buyer must be sure that he or she only pays for what is replaced and must not pay for 100 percent of a tool if only 67 percent of it is worn out.

## Use of the Tool

Can the supplier use this tool to make parts for other customers? Buyers must take steps to protect themselves. This is a point to be negotiated. It has happened that a buyer has paid for a tool, did not protect himself, and the supplier made parts for the buyer's competitors, and then, when the tool wore out, the buyer paid for the new tool!

## Destruction

Finally, when the end of the "life" of a tool comes, who has the authority to destroy it? Again, buyers must take steps to protect themselves. Even if the seller has title to the tool, the buyer can negotiate a clause that the seller must have written authorization from the buyer before the tool is destroyed. Major problems can occur. For example, a very good customer calls up the buyer's company and wants to buy a part to replace a broken one. The buyer calls his or her supplier to order one piece and learns that the supplier destroyed the tool and cannot produce that part. Now, the buyer has two unpleasant options: tell the customer he or she cannot be helped and make the customer very angry, or pay for a brand new tool just to get one part. Either way, the costs are very high to the buyer. This item is overlooked many times in the negotiation process.

## Storage, Insurance, Taxes, and Handling Costs

These four costs are involved whenever tooling is needed to produce a part. They are negotiable. Sellers often do not consider these or ask that the buyer pay them. These are real costs; someone has to absorb them. All tools must be stored somewhere, and factory space is very expensive. And we all would expect to have insurance to pay for a new tool if the old one was destroyed in a fire or by neglect. Also, many states have personal property taxes that must be paid each year on the value of all property, including tools. Even handling costs can be negotiated. This may be a very fertile area for salespeople. This is especially true if the buyer has title to the tool. The seller can state that since the buyer owns the tool, the buyer should pay these costs associated with *his or her* property.

## Setup Charges

There is usually a significant cost to setting up a tool in a machine and then taking the tool out of the machine after the required number of parts have been produced. Since the number of setups is directly related to the number of orders and the amount of parts ordered each time, the seller can take the position that the buyer should pay. The buyer can resist on the grounds that he or she cannot control the labor. Another point to be considered might be whether this is a fixed charge or a charge based upon actual time. If it is based upon actual time, the buyer should require documents to prove the time as well as a control procedure to assure that the buyer only pays for what he gets.

## Rental

If the part is a standard one, the buyer may want to negotiate an agreement that the tool be used to produce parts for other companies, and the buyer be paid a royalty or rental fee. It is very possible that the buyer's total tool cost could be picked up by others. Essentially, in this case, the tool would be free to the buyer.

## Photography

In some cases, especially when dealing with government agencies, a photograph of the tool must be taken to assure that the tool exists and for future identification. Who pays the cost of the photograph is negotiable and could become important if a buyer must have several photographs taken each year.

## Amortization

Many times a buyer wants to establish a second source for a part, but the buyer's company does not have the funds to pay for another tool. A deal may be worked out in which some of the price of the finished part is allocated toward the cost of the tool. For example, a buyer is buying a part for $10.90 from supplier X. Supplier Y quoted $10.27, but a tool must be made. A deal can be arranged in which supplier Y charges $10.90 for each part *and* pays for the tool. For each part produced $.63 is credited toward the cost of the tool. When the tool is paid for, the price for each part drops to $10.27. Buyers must assure that they keep good records so that the seller does not "forget" to lower the price. Sellers must get a solid guarantee that the buyer will purchase enough parts so that the cost of the tool is completely paid for. Here is an issue where both sides can win. In this example, the buyer and seller may agree on a price of $10.77. The buyer reports an immediate cost reduction of $.13 per part and the seller breaks into a new account (and the new account pays for the tool). Later, the buyer can report another cost reduction ($.50 per part) when the tool is paid for.

## Guaranteed Production

During the discussions of tooling, the buyer must establish and get a commitment from the seller for the minimum number of pieces that can be expected to be produced by the tool. This is very important. Very few buyers ever negotiate this point. When we buy something for ourselves as individuals, we generally equate price to expected life of the product. Part of the total cost of any part produced by a tool must be a proportionate share of the original tool cost.

Few buyers will make this type of evaluation: Supplier A is quoting $20,000 for tooling, with expected production of 100,000 parts, and a price of $9.00 per part, therefore, total cost per part is $9.20. Supplier B is quoting $18,000 for tooling, with expected production of 54,000 parts, and a price of $8.90 per part, therefore, total cost of $9.23 per part. Supplier A is offering the best buy even though its tooling cost and apparent price per part is higher then the competition's.

## Approval and Cost of Samples

This is another area in which many buyers do not do an adequate job of negotiating. Most of the time, a buyer pays for a new tool after a few (sometimes as few as six) samples are approved. This is poor procedure. It is possible that the supplier will produce 100 parts and pick the best 15 to send for sample approval. The tool may not be adequate. Or perhaps it is necessary to make 100 parts every time to get 15 acceptable parts. The buyer should negotiate that tool approval (and payment) will only be given after one, two, or three production runs are successfully completed.

A four-cavity die provides another example. The best way to make a die, for the longest possible life, is to make all dimensions on the low side. As the die wears the dimensions will get larger, but still meet the drawing. It could be possible that three out of four cavities are really too low and only one is within tolerances. A supplier could ship 15 samples, all from the same die cavity, to get tooling approval. If approved, the parts from the other three cavities would not meet the drawing for some time. Buyers must get samples from all cavities whenever they have a multicavity die. At the beginning of this chapter the statement was made that price is only one factor in a buyer-seller negotiation. As you review the points discussed since, it should be obvious that each has a lot of potential to provide money (hard, cold cash) to your side of the negotiation table. It bears repeating that it is possible to win the price issue and lose the total negotiation. The professional picks up a lot of "loose change" on issues that he or she is prepared to negotiate and the opponent is not ready to negotiate. It cannot be emphasized too strongly that many issues must be considered during the planning stage of a negotiation. The more you negotiate the greater your chances are of doing very well.

## FOREIGN PURCHASE ISSUES

Whenever the negotiation involves purchasing a part in one country and shipping it to a second country, many points must be considered. It is also very common to negotiate in one country, manufacture the part in a second country, and have it delivered to a third country. The following 16 subheadings cover the major issues to be negotiated.

## Customs Duties/Import Taxes

Customs duties are really import taxes. These are costs that must be paid to an agent of the country into which the material is being delivered. For many items, this tax can be very expensive. It is possible for the import tax to be greater than the value of the goods being imported. This could be a large cost and must be negotiated.

## Import-Export License

An export license is an authorization from the country of origin to ship a product to a second country. In general, the cost of the license is not large, but the costs to get a license may be very, very high. Usually, the responsibility to get this license falls on the seller's shoulders. But who will pay the actual cost to obtain the license? Many sellers may not be considering this issue and are losing the opportunity to gain much in their negotiations. Why not suggest that the buyer pay these costs on an actual-time basis? The seller keeps track of all the hours involved and charges the buyer on a standard cost per hour.

## Banking or Loan Credits/Letter of Credit

Letters of credit are just that. They establish that the customer has the ability to purchase and pay for the item the customer is negotiating. Again, the cost is low, but the cost to obtain a letter of credit might be very high.

## Exchange Rate

The exchange rate that will apply to any order, and the currency that will be used for the transactions, have to be given top priority. The value of any country's currency will vary each day as compared to all other currencies. This point is one on which one side may win price but the other wins the negotiation.

## Cost Insurance Freight

Cost insurance freight (CIF) can best be described with an example. If a buyer purchases a machine in Spain to be delivered to Pittsburgh, Pennsylvania, the buyer could negotiate CIF, New York City. That would mean that the supplier would pay all the costs to move the machine from the vendor's plant to New York City. The vendor would also have title to the machine and the responsibility for insurance. The buyer would then pay for the movement from New York City to Pittsburgh. A large difference in total cost paid by the two sides would happen if the CIF point was Madrid.

## Freight Along Side (FAS)

If the machine in the above example was negotiated to be freight along side (FAS) Lisbon, it would mean that the vendor would pay the transportation costs to the dock at the side of the ship. All other costs and responsibilities would be the buyer's.

What exactly does FAS mean? Does it mean at the exact side of the ship, or does it mean at the dock, or does it mean in the port area? This could cost the buyer a large amount if this point is not clarified. For example, a ship was going to transport the product across the ocean but could not get to the dock, so a smaller vessel was used to take the product from the dock to the ship that was in the harbor. The terms were FAS. Who should pay for the smaller vessel? In this case, the buyer paid a very large sum of money.

## Broker/Paperwork Costs

A broker is a person who assists the buyer, especially with the paperwork and expediting the physical movement of the material. There are costs involved that could be negotiable. The buyer can take the position that the seller should pay these costs and handle all the extra paperwork. When the buyer buys in his or her own country, this is not a factor, so to make all suppliers equal (in the evaluation process) the seller should absorb these costs.

## Inland Transportation/Ocean Transportation/ Special Freight Costs

These items are also very important when negotiating a foreign purchase. Costs are covered by CIF and FAS. The mode of transportation and the route of transportation must also be discussed. Because of the many political considerations involved, this cannot be left to chance. For example, during the summer of 1980, it would not have been too difficult for a buyer in Switzerland to buy some rugs in Karachi, Pakistan, move them by truck across Iran, Iraq, Syria, Turkey, and other countries to Switzerland. An American buyer would have had no real choice except to go by ocean, probably around Africa, to Marseilles, then by land to Switzerland.

The same is true of water routes. At certain times in the past, the Suez Canal was "off limits" for many shippers. Since the route and/ or mode of transportation might be "nonstandard," the seller should take the position that the buyer should pay any special freight costs involved.

## Overseas Packing

Overseas packing is another money issue that can be overlooked. During the 1960s, many buyers became involved for the first time in overseas buying. They had no knowledge of the details involved. There were cases where a buyer was told that any item shipped overseas must have very special packing and that the cost was 10 percent of the value of the product. Since the buyers could not dispute this, the buyers paid. One extreme example was a machine purchased with a value of $527,000 and a packing extra of $27,000 (only 5 percent). The actual cost of materials and labor was $9,000, so the vendor made a profit of $18,000 only because the buyer did not negotiate that issue well.

## Ship Registry

Even what country the ship is registered in should be discussed. In some countries (Liberia and Panama for example), it is easier and somewhat cheaper to register a ship. If this is the case, perhaps the buyer can get a small discount. Also, certain ships may not be allowed to dock or unload at certain ports.

## Which Laws Apply

This is a point that might be a consequence in only one out of 100,000 negotiations, but if it is important it has major consequences. For example, if a buyer in the United States buys steel in Japan, which country's laws apply to the purchase order? If there is a dispute, which court has jurisdiction? Business laws in the United States are very different from those in Japan. A negotiator must assure that a written agreement is made as to which laws apply to the purchase order. In the United States laws also vary from state to state, so the state should be designated.

## Local Content

This refers to local purchases by a vendor when shipment is made to that country. In general, the higher the local content, the more problems the vendor has—and these problems can be significant. When dealing with a government agency in a foreign country, this point could become very important. The government could require that a certain percentage of the product be purchased within the country. A very good example is a power plant. The government will demand that $X$ percent of the plant be purchased in their country. Another very good example is a transportation system.

## Default Procedure/Cancellation and Claims Procedure

To cancel an order in the buyer's own country is usually not much trouble. But when buying overseas, this could become a major problem. This contingency should be covered. It sounds illogical to discuss how to "get out of" a contract before a contract has been agreed to. But it is always important.

## Political Climate/Force Majeure

"Force majeure" means greater force. Parties to a contract can use this concept to excuse themselves from fulfilling their contractual obligations. "Acts of God," war, and so forth are general reasons a supplier may list under a force majeure clause. Buyers must negotiate what is allowed and what is *not* allowed under this clause. If not, the buyer is giving the seller a blank check to get out of any contract the seller wants to at no cost to the seller, *but* at a high cost to the buyer.

## Free Trade Zone/Duty-Free Port/Drawbacks

When doing international business it is possible to make use of free trade areas or duty-free ports to reduce costs and the amount of paperwork. This is especially true for shipments to a third country. A win-win situation can be developed, so buyers and sellers should both explore these points. The cost might be less, so the buyer's price is lower. Since the reduced cost does not hurt the seller, the seller's profit is the same. If the whole product cannot be protected, some of the parts or the raw materials might be protected under a drawback procedure in which duties are not paid on material reshipped out of the country.

## Foreign Shipping Credits

Many suppliers will reduce their price on materials to be used in products that will be shipped outside the United States. The idea is that any new sales will add labor hours of work for American workers. The unions at some of these suppliers will agree to special conditions on such material. Their major interest is to increase U.S. labor hours at the expense of foreign labor. Any buyer who is shipping outside the United States should pursue this point very strenuously. There may be more paperwork, but it could be worth it. This ends the discussion of the most important issues to be negotiated if the transaction will involve two different countries. Others may occur to readers involved in particular negotiations.

## DISCOUNT TIME/DISCOUNT PERCENTAGE

It is standard practice to give a discount to a customer who pays bills promptly. Terms of one percent/10–30 days is most common. Today, with the cost of money so high, a cash discount can become very important. The negotiator must remember that both the percentage and the number of days is negotiable.

A ploy used by many sellers is to say that their company policy is one percent/10-net 30 and that that policy must apply. This is just a negotiating tactic. Each day many hundreds or even thousands of companies are reviewing policies for the purpose of revising them, rewriting them, dropping them, and so forth. A company policy is not written in concrete forever. Most growing, dynamic, prosperous companies change policies often to keep the policies current and to have them meet current needs.

Another ploy is "industry practice," that is, to argue that everyone is offering the same terms, so the buyer must accept them. Again, industry practices change. For example, before 1920, a 48-hour workweek was standard practice (eight hours a day, six days a week). Today, it is not the standard. Buyers should also make the point that all companies in one industry do not have to charge the same terms. As a matter of fact, it could be illegal for sellers to agree to charge the same terms.

## Free on Board/Freight Allowed or Not Allowed/Collect-Prepaid

These three items cover normal transportation points. "FOB" stands for Free on Board. The significance is that this is where the title passes. If a vendor quotes FOB shipping point, it means that the buyer has title to the material from the time it leaves the vendor's plant. "FOB destination" means the vendor has title until it arrives and is unloaded at the buyer's plant. Normally, this is not important, but it could be. Two examples will demonstrate the importance of this point. If a truck catches fire and the material is destroyed, whoever has the title must make the insurance claim. This can involve a lot of work and the owner's money is generally tied up for months.

Or, if anyone is hurt in an accident involving the material, the owner of the material could be sued. The classic case is a coil of steel that rolls off a flat bed truck and kills a small child. The child's family sues both the trucker and the buyer (it was FOB shipping point).

The FOB point and who pays the freight costs do not have to be the same. If it is FOB shipping point, the buyer can still negotiate for the vendor to pay the cost of transportation. The other side of the coin is also true. Buyer can pay transportation costs even if it is FOB destination.

"Freight allowed" means that the vendor does not make an extra charge on the invoice. In theory, the vendor is absorbing these costs.

"Not allowed" means the buyer must pay the transportation costs.

"Collect-prepaid" only determines who pays the transportation bill. Just because one side pays the bill does not mean that side *must* absorb the cost.

There are several combinations of these terms, as described below.

*Prepaid and freight allowed.*   Supplier pays carrier and absorbs freight charges. Most advantageous unless supplier has obviously included freight in the price.

*Collect and freight allowed.*   Supplier absorbs charges, but buyer must audit and pay carrier freight bill, and check the supplier invoice to assure correct freight allowance. If supplier is to absorb freight, buyer should insist on *prepaid* shipments.

*Collect and freight not allowed.*   Buyer audits and pays carrier freight bill and absorbs the expense. If buyer must absorb freight, many suggest that shipments should be received *collect* for obvious audit and control reasons. Invoice only includes product cost.

*Prepaid and freight not allowed.*   Supplier pays carrier bill and adds to invoice, so buyer must audit invoice to assure accuracy of freight charge additions. Should never be used except where Parcel Post or UPS are used since it is extremely difficult to control and verify charges unless a carrier's bill accompanies the supplier's invoice.

## RAIL DEMURRAGE/TRUCK DETENTION

Carriers allow shippers and receivers a specified amount of time in which loading and/or unloading must be accomplished. Detention of the equipment beyond the free-time allowance will result in penalty charges where the delay is not caused by the carrier. Thus, the buyer must load and unload as promptly as possible. In general, these costs would be paid by the owner. But what if the vendor shipped early or late and the buyer's plant cannot unload because of other railroad cars or trucks?

*Rail demurrage.*   Railroads allow 48 hours of free time for loading and unloading rail cars. The free time begins at 7:00 A.M. after the car is placed at the siding. Saturdays, Sundays, and holidays are excluded. Someone will be charged for each day of delay after free time expires at a rate of approximately $10 per day for the first four days, approximately $20 per day for the next four days, and approximately $30 per day for every day thereafter. Heavy-duty flats and certain special-purpose cars carry a detention charge in addition to the normal demurrage charges. The bill will go to the buyer, but who absorbs the cost is up for negotiation.

*Truck detention.*   Free time for loading and unloading truck shipments (where the driver is waiting) varies with the carrier and the size of the shipment. Practically all carriers require a certain amount of time in which large truckload shipments must be loaded or unloaded. For example, on truckload shipments weighing between 20,000–30,000-pounds, trailers must generally be loaded or unloaded within four hours. The buyer can be assessed as much as $20 for each hour the equipment is held beyond the free-time allowance.

At some locations, when shipping via certain motor carriers, shipments of the less-truckload and small-lot category must be loaded or unloaded within 30–45 minutes.

Depending on the territory, 24–48 hours of free time are provided for loading or unloading trailers which have been "dropped" or "spotted." Charges for holding the trailers beyond the free time is comparable to the rail demurrage charges.

Every effort should be made to schedule pickups, deliveries, and equipment placement so that loading and unloading will be prompt. In return, the buyer expects the cooperation of all carriers to meet its shipping and receiving needs.


## FREIGHT EQUALIZATION

A major goal for the buyer in every negotiation and purchase of any item is to have the supplier absorb the transportation costs without adjusting the selling price, or have all suppliers quote selling price with transportation included. The latter, of course, to be accepted only where it is customary within an industry or where it is obviously advantageous to the buyer.

The next possibility is to require the supplier to equalize transportation with a competitive supplier. The nearest competitive supply point would govern the maximum amount of transportation which the buyer would absorb, and any differences would be borne by the competing suppliers.

The system of freight equalization is usually practiced within the steel and chemical industries. In industries where it is not, an attempt could be made to either acquire such an equalization arrangement or to receive advantages in other areas of negotiation. For example see Figure 5-4.

Other factors being equal, the purchase should be made from the Cleveland supplier because of the lower freight rate. However, the Chicago supplier could participate by equalizing the transportation by one of two methods:

1. FOB P/S, Collect, Freight Equalized with Cleveland, OH. (Chicago supplier would ship collect *and* buyer would pay the carrier $123.50 (5,000 lbs @ $2.47). Chicago supplier would deduct $48.00 (5,000 lbs @ $.96) from the invoice, which is the difference between the Chicago and Cleveland rates.

2. FOB P/S, Prepaid, Freight Equalized with Cleveland, OH. (Chicago supplier would ship prepaid and add $75.50 (5,000 lbs @ $1.51) to the invoice, which is the rate from Cleveland.

---

Requirement: 5,000 lbs. of iron or steel machine parts to be delivered to Pittsburgh.
Available suppliers:  A Chicago supplier
                         A Cleveland supplier
Normal delivery terms of both suppliers: FOB P/S Collect, Freight Not Allowed
Truck rates:

| | Chicago | | |
|---|---|---|---|
| | | Cleveland | |
| | $2.47/cwt | $1.51/cwt | Pittsburgh |

---

**Figure 5-4**   Freight equalization

The buyer must audit the supplier's invoice to assure the accuracy of freight added or deducted (depending on who pays the carrier) from a named equalization point. This should be attempted in all cases of supplier competition and, where successful, the supplier should prepay shipments and add the freight from the point of equalization to the invoice.

## TRANSPORTATION ROUTE, TRANSPORTATION MODE, AND SUPPLIER

The method of shipment or the selection of a carrier is directly dependent upon the size and weight of the shipment and the service required. Buyers should consult their companies' traffic departments on inbound routings where traffic personnel are available, before negotiating with potential suppliers.

Each buying location and each individual supplier operates under different carrier and transportation circumstances. Consequently, a single set of routing rules for uniform application is impractical for this discussion. The statements that follow list the different transportation methods which are generally available.

*Air freight.* Handled by regular passenger airlines and air freight carriers. Pickup and delivery is available. More costly than truck, rail, freight forwarder, REA Express, and parcel post. On occasion, may be delayed to give priority to mail or air express.

*Air freight forwarder.* A company whose service includes pickup and delivery and transportation on most all commercial airlines. Slightly higher in cost than air freight in most cases. Usually moves in space allotted and may receive priority to regular air freight.

*Air express.* Complete service including pickup and delivery by all commercial airlines. More costly than air freight on shipments weighing over approximately 50 pounds. Air freight service is comparable to major cities.

*Air parcel post.* Fourth class airmail. Costs less than air express up to approximately 15 pounds. Generally not advisable on valuable shipments where delivery is urgent.

*Bus.*    Handled in regular bus baggage compartments. Pickup and delivery service is not available. More costly than truck, rail, and freight forwarder when over approximately 70 pounds. Difficult to trace if lost. Valuable shipments should move via different carriers.

*Parcel post.*    Fourth class regular mail. Less expensive than REA Express or bus. Used on small packages of little value on which delivery is not urgent.

*Carload or truckload.*    Full railcar or trailer. Lowest cost. Total charges depend on minimum weight required and other factors.

*Truck.*    Less than truckload (LTL). Economical method of shipping over approximately 50 pounds and is used to transport most materials and products.

Both buyers and sellers must be aware of the fact that, pound for pound, the transportation charges for small shipments exceed the charges of medium to large shipments by roughly 50–75 percent. A shipment weighing less than 75–100 pounds may be considered small and very costly. Every effort should be made to increase order quantities and sizes so as to reduce the number of small shipment receipts.

Although transportation is somewhat regulated by the government, rates and charges are actually established by the various carriers on the basis of shipper needs subject to certain variables, some of which are: distance, commodity characteristics (value, size, weight, density, etc.), claim experience, and volume of movement. Rate negotiation is one of the many areas that must be considered. Ideally, the more beneficial terms should only be conceded to possible advantages in other areas of the negotiation.

## CONSOLIDATION OF FREIGHT/NUMBER OF ITEMS PER SHIPMENT/EXCLUSIVE USE OF TRUCK OR RAILROAD CAR

These points will particularly be negotiable factors if small quantities are shipped on a regular basis. The cost factor and the speed of delivery will be the most important areas to consider.

## PARTIAL PAYMENT OF FREIGHT

Buyers might attempt to negotiate a contract in which the supplier pays part of the freight costs for every day that the material is late after a specified time. A sliding scale can be established such as:

Normal time: Three-day delivery

Fourth-day delivery: Supplier pays 10% of cost

Fifth-day delivery: Supplier pays 25% of cost

## REPAIR TO IN-TRANSIT DAMAGE

The FOB negotiation determines who is responsible for the costs to repair material damaged during transit from the supplier to the buyer. Another question that must be discussed is, if repairs are needed, who makes them, how will they be accomplished, who approves them, and so forth. An example occurred a few years ago when a truckload of refrigerators tipped over. Many were damaged. A local fix-it shop was given the order to repaint several of them. They were then shipped to the buyer, who rejected them. After several trips out and back, the paint job was finally acceptable. Since it was FOB destination, the buyer did not have to pay anything. The buyer lost, however, because the refrigerators were not in his store for several weeks and potential customers went to his competitors.

From the buying side, even if the terms are FOB destination, the buyer must be concerned about repair to materials damaged in transit. The buyer might negotiate that all repairs are to be done only in places approved by the buyer. The buyer might take complete responsibility for repairs and charge-back the seller when they are complete.

Sellers should not overlook this point even though the problem may not come up very often. Buyers will easily forget the 100 shipments delivered without problems if one shipment is damaged and handled poorly. Sellers should push for FOB shipping point and let the buyer worry about in-transit damage.

## PREMIUM TRANSPORTATION

When a supplier is late or when the buyer needs material faster than normal, premium transportation might be used. If the normal method of shipment is railcar, a truck might be used. If the normal method is truck, air might be used. This is generally referred to as premium transportation.

Buyers should be aware of a couple of points. First, if the supplier is late or has had a problem, the buyer's position should be that the supplier pays for the total freight bill. Second, if the buyer requested the premium transportation, the buyer should get a rebate on the price, especially if the terms were prepaid and allowed. The supplier has included some freight costs in the price. Since the supplier will not have to pay these costs, the savings should be passed on to the buyer.

If this issue is negotiated before the transportation is needed it is best for both sides. Generally when a major problem happens, neither side is ready to discuss it on a rational basis. The "ground rules" for premium transportation is an issue to be considered during your planning.

## QUANTITY/LOT SIZE/OVER AND UNDER

There is no question that quantity will be discussed, but two other concepts are important. The size of each shipment (lot size) can affect costs very significantly. Most businesses find certain lot sizes are more economical than others. The seller should attempt to negotiate an agreement with the buyer that allows the seller to ship in economical lot sizes. This may not be too important to the buyer. It could, however, make a big difference to the seller. "Over and under" refers to the deviation allowed from the quantity ordered. For example, if a buyer orders 100,000 pounds of steel, what constitutes a complete shipment? Some industries have a $\pm$ 10 percent deviation. If this were the case with steel, the seller could ship anywhere from 90,000–110,000 pounds and call the order complete. That is a 20 percent range. From the buying side, this might be too large. A large range can cause major problems for a buyer.

If the market is very tight and business is very strong, the seller will ship 90,000 pounds and call the order complete. If the seller does this for 10 customers, he or she can take care of an eleventh customer "free." None of the 11 customers received exactly what they ordered, but all orders are complete. Buyers now have to place another order, which will usually not be shipped for several weeks, and the buyer's plant may run out of this material. On the other hand, if the market is weak and business is very slow, the seller will be tempted to ship 110,000 pounds and call the order complete. The buyer now has an inventory overage and the buyer's costs will go up. At the same time, the seller has increased his or her GSB in the short term. If the seller does this for all customers, the seller gets a "free" 10 percent increase in sales. It is true that the next order from the buyer will be delayed, but perhaps by that time the market will be getting stronger.

In either case (10 percent over or 10 percent under), the buyer suffered more than the seller did. This issue is very negotiable even if the "industry standard" is $X$ percent.

## RESEARCH AND DEVELOPMENT

This item offers great potential for the buyer. Many companies have an R&D department. The size of this department may vary from one or two people to 400–500 people. For a business to continue to grow and stay competitive, meaningful effort must be directed toward R&D. This effort costs money. In general, the salaries, overhead, and other costs in an R&D department are higher than in any other department in the company.

The R&D departments are where the PhD.s and Master's degree holders are employed. Who pays for the R&D department? Customers pay for it. Some part of each dollar of GSB goes to pay for R&D. Every time a buyer pays an invoice, he or she is paying toward R&D work.

Buyers should negotiate to get *direct* value for the money they are spending for their supplier's R&D. No one formula will fit all situations, but a good starting point is two percent of purchases. For example, assume that a buyer is spending $727,000 per year with one company and that a research day costs $200. The buyer should point out that he or she is paying $14,540 toward the supplier's R&D. The buyer then negotiates that 72 days per year of a research person's time be dedicated to projects that the buyer determines. That way the buyer is getting full value for his or her money.

Industrial buyers often complain that their engineering department will not test their cost-reduction ideas or approve new suppliers, and so forth. A buyer who can negotiate $X$ days of research time can have the supplier test the buyer's cost-reduction ideas. The buyer will then have a very strong case to take to top management and be able to force engineering to approve. (Of course, the testing company must be in a different industry than the company being tested.)

The buyers' position during the negotiation process is simple, but strong. Buyers should make these points: (1) that they are paying $X$ dollars to support the supplier's R&D department; (2) that the supplier's people have to do something, so why not work on projects for customer's projects which might easily get the company future business; and (3) that at $Y$ cost per day, the buyers should have $Z$ days per year of R&D time.

Control of such a program is simple. Time cards and progress reports are sent weekly (monthly if the total value is low) to the buyer.

## PATENTS/COPYRIGHTS/PROPRIETARY INFORMATION/USE OF TRADEMARK/USE OF DRAWINGS/USE OF CONFIDENTIAL INFORMATION/USE OF COMPANY DATA

All of these items should be negotiated by the salesteam. If a buyer wants to use any of them, it should "cost" the buyer something—either actual money or issues in the negotiation. There is a generally a lot of cost entailed in these items. For example, obtaining a patent is a slow and costly process. The buyer should be expected to pay *directly* for the use of a patent or copyright information.

Use of a trademark falls into the same category. If the buyer asks to use a seller's trademark, the buyer must feel that he or she will benefit. If the buyer is going to benefit, the seller should receive a part of it, even though it is "free advertising" for the seller. But sellers must remember that this is an opportunity to gain in a negotiation. A good ploy would be to offer to let the buyer use the trademark if the buyer agrees to something the seller wants. This way, the seller gains.

On the other hand a seller often wants to use buyers' trademarks in his or her advertising. When the buyer is asked for permission, the buyer is in a perfect position to gain another issue in the negotiation or an IOU to be cashed later. Buyers can take advantage of some of these points.

For example, a buyer tests a supplier's material for vendor approval. The test results show that the material is acceptable. The supplier is approved. This information can be very valuable to the seller. The seller can take the data and show it to other potential customers: "Here are objective test results of our materials. Our material will work in your application. With this data, you can save test time." The seller can get more business for little cost, and a customer can get better material for little cost, all because of the information developed from the buyer's testing of the material. If the seller wants to see or get a copy of the information, the seller should "pay." The first position that the buyer should take is that it costs $X$ dollars to conduct these tests, so the seller should pay $X$ dollars if he or she wants a copy of the results. From that position, the buyer has many options open for negotiation.

The purpose of these seven issues concerning information is that, as a negotiator, you should never give away anything. If the other side wants something (or even indicates an interest in something) it will "cost" them. This cost might be dollars and cents, concession of another issue, or it might be saved as a future IOU.

## SUPPLIER'S SUPPLIERS (SUBTIER COMPANIES)/ SUBCONTRACT RIGHTS/AUTHORIZATION TO VISIT AT SUBTIER/USE MINORITY VENDORS/USE SMALL BUSINESS/USE BUSINESS FROM DEPRESSED AREAS

A buyer can insist that he or she be part of vendor's decisions as to who the vendor will buy from. In many cases, this is very important. Suppliers should never have the right to subcontract a complete order to another manufacturer without the agreement of the buyer. But if the buyer does not make this part of the negotiation, the buyer cannot stop this practice. If a seller wants the flexibility of being able to subcontract an order, the seller should expect to pay for this flexibility. It is possible for a buyer to have major problems with a supplier and remove the supplier from the buyer's approved list, only to find later that that supplier is still doing work for the buyer's company (as a subcontractor).

Many companies have significant goals for increasing the amount of business they are placing with minority vendors, smaller businesses, and business from labor-depressed areas. These companies can negotiate that their vendors use similar suppliers. Many companies report this information.

The seller should always be open to discussion on these issues. The seller must stress that using a supplier other than its regular sources of supply will probably cost money and that the buyer should expect to pay the extra costs. For example, if a company must maintain inventory for two different suppliers for the same part, the total inventory will be larger than maintaining the inventory for one supplier of that part. Two purchase orders must be negotiated, placed, administered, and so forth. In many other areas, the cost increases. This cost is negotiable and the seller should be able to quote this cost whenever a buyer opens the discussion on these points.

## SPARE PARTS/REPLACEMENT PARTS/RENEWAL PARTS

These three issues represent an area in which a buyer can save his or her company a lot of money in the future. (When a buyer tabulates the results of a negotiation, the buyer must include the future savings in this area.) These terms are differentiated as follows.

"Spart parts" are parts sent with the original order. For instance, if a buyer purchased a punch press, any extra parts on the same purchase order would be spare parts. Some parts of a machine wear out faster than the machine itself. Buyers will get a list of these parts and buy some with the machine.

"Renewal parts" are parts purchased after the machine is delivered, to replace parts that wear out on a regular basis.

"Replacement parts" are parts that wear out or break that are not expected to do so. These fall into the "surprise" area. In general, renewal parts and replacement parts cost much more than spare parts. Many times, this cost is two to five times higher. Spare parts generally cost more than the same part does in the machine.

An article in the July 10, 1980, issue of *The Wall Street Journal* illustrates this point.

> *Expensive Wrecks. The Alliance of American Insurers, a trade group, says a new study shows it would cost $24,458 in parts and labor to replace all parts on a totally wrecked 1980 U.S. compact auto that cost the dealer $6,018.**

A few years ago, this same type of result occurred in a study in which someone purchased all the parts for one model car from more than 30 different dealers. The cost of the parts alone was four times the cost of the same car assembled and ready to drive. The point is that there is a very large markup on spare, replacement, and renewal parts. Many industries make more profit from the sale of parts (the "aftermarket") than they do from the original sale of the equipment. An aggressive buyer should negotiate these items, and try to fix the future costs of parts. The buyer can start with a parts list and a cost analysis of each part. The buyer must then negotiate a price schedule for future delivery of these items.

A significant amount of money can be saved by negotiating these issues. This is particularly true if the seller is not prepared to negotiate. During the negotiation for a large machine, when the seller is hungry for the order, the buyer has a good chance to get concessions on these issues. After the seller has the order, the buyer has no leverage at all.

When a part breaks on your car, you generally have three options: replace the part; buy a new car; or ride with someone else. The third option is troublesome, requires coordination efforts, results in lack of freedom, and so forth and is seldom the choice made. Comparing options one and two, option one is always the lowest cost. Only when the car is very old and the owner decides it is not worth it to invest in this "old clunker" anymore does the owner pick option two. In general replacing the part is the best option. This is true if the cost of the part is X dollars, 2X dollars, or 3X dollars. The fact is, you are a captive of the repair service. It is very difficult to negotiate. The repair service can take the position of take it or leave it. It is impossible in most cases to justify these extra costs. But buyers should always try to negotiate these issues.

## BREAK-IN PARTS

With certain pieces of equipment several parts may be used up or completely consumed during the start-up process. In addition, on many machines some items will be used at a more rapid rate during the first few months of operation—the break-in period. Buyers should protect themselves on this issue. The actual cost of a piece of equipment might be higher than planned during the first year or so of operation. The prices and amount of break-in parts should be fixed. If the machine does not get started on schedule and more parts are needed, why should the buyer pay more?

## MATERIAL CONSUMED DURING BREAK-IN PERIOD

With some machines, productive material is used and becomes scrap during the break-in period. This is part of the cost of the machine. As such, it is a negotiable item. As with break-in parts, a buyer should try to get the supplier to pay all or part of this cost, and the buyer must try to establish a maximum cost above which the supplier will pay all costs.

The seller will usually take the position that since the buyer is controlling the break-in of a new machine or the largest part of the break-in, the seller cannot assume any responsibility for these costs. Then the negotiation will begin.

We are now approximately half-way through the list of issues to be considered in a buyer-seller negotiation. The first 123 issues were very detailed. Some readers may feel that they were too detailed. For example, why divide spare, replacement, and renewal parts into three different items?

The list is detailed because of the relationship between planning and winning a negotiation. Too often, one negotiator forgets an issue. For example, the negotiator may plan for and negotiate spare parts and replacement parts, but forget renewal parts. If so, the opponent could gain a lot. The more detailed the plan, the greater the probability of success.

Research indicates that many negotiators do not get into the "nuts and bolts" or the "nitty-gritty" of planning. This research indicates that these negotiators will lose most of their negotiations. There is absolutely no substitute for a complete planning job. The negotiator must be prepared to commit the time to do it.

Remember, it is a truism of negotiations that if one side is prepared to negotiate an issue and the other side is not prepared, the prepared side will almost always win that issue. Another point to reinforce is that when each issue is reviewed in this book, examples are given to illustrate that issue. Many other examples could be given. If the example is from the buyer's side, examples could be given where the seller's side can gain. Either side in a negotiation can win any issue in that negotiation. That is why the negotiator must be prepared on every issue to be discussed in the negotiation.

## QUALITY/WARRANTY (LABOR, SERVICE, PARTS AND MATERIALS, TIME, NEW WARRANTY BASED ON NEW WORK)/SPECIFICATION/ACCEPTABLE QUALITY LEVELS

Several books have been written about the subject of quality, so an in-depth review is not required here. The most important aspect from the negotiation viewpoint is to negotiate the correct quality level. This means not too low, but also not too high a quality level. Many times the buyer pays the "right price" for an item that is "too good." An important concept is the relationship of price and function.

Warranty is an important item and buyers must remember to negotiate so that the warranty only starts when the product is used. When you buy a car, the warranty starts when you drive the car off of the dealer's lot. How would you feel if one week after purchasing a new car something was not right and you went back to the dealer for help and the dealer said the warranty is over. You would be most unhappy. Especially if the dealer said, "The warranty was 12 months or 12,000 miles, and since this car was manufactured 13 months ago the warranty is over." When you buy a car, major appliance, and so forth, you expect the warranty to start when you begin using the product.

Many times in industrial buying situations the warranty starts when the material arrives, not when it is used. It is most embarrassing for a buyer to have a product fail in his factory and have no recourse with the supplier because the warranty ran out. Acceptable quality levels (AQL) refers to the statistical method for checking material. If a buyer buys 100,000 bolts, the buyer's company will not inspect all 100,000 items. Some method will be used to check a sample of the shipment. During negotiations, the method and the sample lot size should be discussed. The higher the level required, the easier it is to use the parts in the buyer's factory. At the same time, the supplier's costs may increase, so there is a significant impact on both sides of the table and both sides should be prepared to negotiate.

## LEARNING CURVE/EXPERIENCE CURVE

This is one of the most powerful tools that a buyer can use during a negotiation. This point will present a factual, logical reason for reduced prices from the seller.

The learning curve concept is simply a provable way of demonstrating that the more a person does anything, the faster the person does it, and generally the higher quality the person's work. This is true of all jobs, both at work and at home. For example, a person packing golf balls into boxes will pack faster the second day the person does it than on the first day. You will cut the grass faster the fifth time than you did the first time.

Various degrees of the concept will apply depending upon the industry the seller represents. It is possible to have a 98 percent learning curve or a 75 percent learning curve. The textbook example is the airplane industry when manufacturing completed airplanes. The effect applies every time production doubles. For example, an 80 percent learning curve would produce the following results.

| Airplane | Total Direct Labor Hours |
|----------|--------------------------|
| 1 | 10,000 |
| 2 | 8,000 |
| 4 | 6,400 |
| 8 | 5,120 |
| 16 | 4,096 |
| 32 | 3,277 |
| 64 | 2,621 |

To demonstrate the importance of the percentage, here is an example of a 90 percent curve:

| Airplane | Total Direct Labor Hours |
|----------|--------------------------|
| 1 | 10,000 |
| 2 | 9,000 |
| 4 | 8,100 |
| 8 | 7,290 |
| 16 | 6,561 |
| 32 | 5,905 |
| 64 | 5,315 |

Note that an 80 percent curve allows 8,000 hours for the second plane, while a 90 percent curve allows about the same number—8,100—for the fourth plane. Buyers will want to negotiate as low a percentage as possible and sellers will aim for as close to 100 percent as possible.

During the negotiation, the buyer will use the learning curve to try to fix direct labor costs for future production. Using the airplane as an example, if a buyer will buy 10 planes a year for seven years, the buyer can negotiate the allowed direct labor hours in the sixty-fourth plane. The buyer can establish a labor rate for today and add an inflation factor. The allowed hours (90 percent curve equals 5,315, see above) times the allowed rate will give the buyer a firm direct labor cost today for a plane that will be delivered in seven years. Many companies have used this concept not only when they are buying, but also when they are developing marketing and business strategies. The learning curve is important in planning, as well as in negotiations, because as a company's product volume and market share increases, costs will also decrease. Lower cost could result in higher volume and even lower cost, until a clear advantage is gained as compared to the competition.

Most people see two related approaches:

1. Manufacturing costs. The learning curve applies to direct labor costs and this proves that manufacturing costs decline as volume increases. Many examples have been developed in industries with standard products.

2. All costs. Some people also look at total costs using this concept. It is called the experience curve. This includes a broader range of costs that also should decline as volume increases.

Three articles from the *Harvard Business Review* provide more information: "The Learning Curve as a Production Tool" (January–February 1954), "Profit from the Learning Curve" (January–February 1964), and "Limits of the Learning Curve" (September–October 1974).

## COST OF SERVICES ANALYSIS/(TYPE OF LABOR, HOURS, RATES, INSURANCE/BONDS)

If *any* services are to be performed by the seller as part of the total contract (or a services contract itself), these items must be negotiated. The type of labor refers to the skill level. There are examples of a contractor using highly paid employees so as to keep them during slow periods, rather than using lower-paid people who would be qualified to complete the job. If the seller wants to use higher skilled people, that is all right, but the pay should be at the appropriate level.

The major question about hours is when they begin. Some companies charge from home to home, some from home to office to home, some from time on customer's property to time off, and some only charge for actual work hours. A considerable amount of money is at stake in this area. It is possible to have work hours be fewer than 50 percent of the hours charged.

Insurance and bonds are listed because either the buyer or the seller must pay for these items and both are negotiable.

## SUPPLIER CAPACITY (MAXIMUM, MINIMUM, GUARANTEED, PROOF OF CAPABILITY, PURCHASED)

It is possible that these issues could be especially important during periods of tight supply. During a buyer's market, a salesperson would often rather win the order than win the negotiation. During a seller's market, a buyer wants to get material.

Capacity can be a most important point. Many companies must work on short lead times from their customers and have constant problems receiving material on time from their suppliers. A capacity negotiation may be the answer. For example, consider the die-cast aluminum industry. The major factors in producing parts is how many times per shift aluminum is "shot" into the die and how many cavities are there in the die. A buyer could negotiate to guarantee so many "shots" per month or so many operating shifts per month. A buyer could say, "I'll guarantee you [seller] six shifts of operation starting the first day of the month on die-cast machine 1. I'll contact you four days before the first of the month and tell you what die to put on the machine first, (for $X$ number of parts), second (for $X$ number of parts), and so forth."

This would reduce the buyer's lead time to less than a week and would help the seller schedule work more effectively. If the buyer did not need any parts and the seller could not make anything else on die-cast machine 1 during those days, the buyer would be responsible for paying for profit lost (only profit, because no material or labor costs would be incurred).

Many other industries can use the same concept. Buyers can help to significantly reduce their companies's lead times to customers. Sellers also should consider this point because it will help their plant's production and scheduling and should add to profit.

## TESTING (EQUIPMENT, DESIGN, COSTS, SOURCE, PRODUCT TESTING, NONPRODUCT TESTING, SPECIAL TESTING, SPECIAL ENVIRONMENT, NONDESTRUCTIVE TESTING)

The area of testing usually provides many points to be negotiated. The basic question is who will perform the testing and who will pay for it. It often happens that one side will do the testing but the other side will pay for it.

It is possible for a supplier not only to test the product he or she is supplying, but also to test products others are supplying, or to test other products. In this area, it is possible for the seller to concede points that have little cost to the seller and high value to the buyer. High creativity in this area can produce big gains for the sales side of the negotiation.

## OBSOLETE MATERIAL/SURPLUS MATERIAL

When the buyer has either obsolete or surplus material in stock, there is an opportunity for gain by both sides. Assuming that the material is in usable condition, the seller may offer to "take it off the buyer's hands" for a reduced price. A very important consideration is the cost of carrying inventory. The seller will want to determine, in advance if possible, the actual rate it costs the buyer's company to carry inventory. Now the seller can make an intelligent offer in which the buyer gains, and the seller pays no more than the seller has to for the material. (The seller can then use the material or resell it for an easy profit.)

## DAMAGED MATERIAL

One seller gained several IOUs with a customer by taking some damaged finished products "off of the buyer's hands." The buyer had been trying to get rid of the material for more than a year. The seller broke even because the seller received just enough value to offset costs. More important were the IOUs.

## TRAINING

The cost of training today is very high. To prepare training programs is very expensive. To develop one hour of presentation takes approximately 10–15 hours of research, writing, and other development work, including practice presentations. Reviewing the many advertising fliers that announce public seminars being offered in all phases of business, you will see that the cost per day for one student is high.

There is considerable value to this negotiation point. If a buyer, for example, could negotiate to have the supplier present a training program at no charge, the buyer's side would gain a lot of value. Either side in a negotiation could have the ability to present training programs. Many large companies have their own in-house education departments. Some even have training centers where students (employees) live, eat, enjoy recreation activities, and attend class. These education departments are staffed with people who are highly qualified in industrial education. Most are experts in their field (engineering, purchasing, marketing, accounting, etc.) as well as being highly skilled teachers. The ability to present an outstanding training program is a unique skill and this skill can bring great value at the negotiation table. The side with this ability can either trade the issue for other valuable issues, or it can sell the service, as a separate product.

There are other benefits to negotiating training as part of the contract, especially from the sales side. In general, when buyers and sellers talk, negotiate, meet, and so forth, the buyer is "on guard." During a training program, the trainer from the seller's company can not only teach, but also do a lot of selling. It must be soft selling, but it is still selling.

Courses to be considered should include, for example, technical courses about the product being bought and sold, general product information courses, business courses, management courses, purchasing courses, sales courses, and accounting courses.

Finally, there is a tremendous value to the employees who attend training programs. Significant emphasis is being placed on human resource development in most companies today. Career development and quality of work life are two important concepts in today's business environment. Meaningful training programs can contribute to both. Human resource development is steadily growing in size and impact. This negotiation issue can bring many side benefits and the negotiator offering the training should receive good value in return.

## TOLERANCES ON DRAWINGS

This is an area which is often overlooked, but has the possibility of yielding great benefits, especially for the buyer's side. If tolerances on drawings are tightened up (from $\pm$ 0.005 to $\pm$ 0.003), the price could go up. If the tolerance is relaxed (from $\pm$ 0.013 to $\pm$ 0.027), the price will generally go down.

Buyers have two opportunities to gain an advantage. First, the buyer should investigate actual needs. Many times the tolerance on the drawing is not required to put the buyer's product together. It is possible to have two parts go together and the tolerances on their respective drawings to be different. In this case, the higher tolerance should be taken. The buyer must determine if production requirements will allow higher tolerance. If so, there is an opportunity for gain. The buyer must, however, be cimcumspect. He or she cannot ask how much will be saved if the tolerance is changed. The seller will be alerted and may say "nothing." So the buyer has to establish beforehand how much will be saved. Later the buyer can propose a change in the tolerance and ask for the appropriate saving.

There is a second opportunity that almost every buyer misses. This opportunity is to tighten up the tolerance. This should shock a buyer. I will have to pay more, the buyer says. But the buyer's company may save, and this is a big "but." If the tolerance on two parts that are held together by a screw is tighter, the parts may go together much faster in the factory. This would increase productivity and save money because the center lines of both parts are aligned. It is very possible that the increased cost on the parts is less than the savings in the factory.

This is truly professional buying, when a buyer checks into these details. Both sides need to be fully prepared to negotiate this issue. Tolerances on the drawing is a perfect example of an issue that can be won by the side that prepared for it. If one side is ready to negotiate and the other has not planned and does not know anything about the details, the prepared side will win and generally win big.

## CANCELLATION PROCEDURES/ESCAPE CLAUSES/ BACK-ORDER PROCEDURES/EXCUSABLE DELAYS/ CANCELLATION COSTS/DEFAULT PROCEDURES/ CHANGE NOTICE PROCEDURE

When negotiating a contract, some people feel it is a poor practice to discuss cancellation of the proposed contract. These people feel that this is negotiating in bad faith. However, it is a *must* to negotiate this issue, and every professional negotiator understands this. No one can precisely forecast the future, let alone predict acts of God, war, fire, and so forth. The negotiator must protect his or her side and include these points in the planning.

## TYPE OF CONTRACT (FIXED PRICE + FIXED FEE, FIXED PRICE + GUARANTEED PROFIT, COST PLUS INCENTIVE FEE)

Listed above are three different types of contracts for examples only. There are many variations and options open to buyers and sellers. The type of contract is a very important point to negotiate.

## GOVERNMENT REGULATIONS (OCCUPATIONAL SAFETY AND HEALTH ACT, PROCUREMENT POLICIES, MILITARY SPECIFICATIONS)

Again these are only three of many different government regulations. If any will affect your negotiation, be sure to plan to negotiate one of them.

## GOVERNMENT PAPERWORK

The cost to complete forms, reports, and so forth for federal, state, and local governments is staggering. This is a very heavy load for all businesses. The cost is also an issue to be negotiated. The more paperwork the other side does for you, the more money your company saves. Many times the negotiator will know the true cost of paperwork to his or her company. You can gain because of this, by asking your opponent to complete all required paperwork. Your opponent could give in, especially if you give a small issue in return.

## EQUAL EMPLOYMENT OPPORTUNITY/MINORITY VENDORS/MINORITY VENDOR PERCENTAGE

Many contracts require that subcontractors comply in these two areas. Each negotiator's responsibility requires that these two issues be negotiated. For most U.S. government orders these two items are must points. A seller could gain significantly if the seller's minority vendor program will also count toward the seller's customers' minority vendor programs. Sellers should check this point. Some orders will require a minimum percentage of minority vendor participation. If the seller exceeds the minimum, the seller should ask for more.

## SHIPPING CONTAINERS/PACKING

These issues are similar to quality. The buyer must assure that the correct packing is used. Too much packing will result in unnecessarily high prices. Too little may cause product damage.

## REJECTION PROCEDURE/SCRAP RETURN PROCEDURE/SCRAP REPAIR PROCEDURE/ MATERIAL REPLACEMENT PROCEDURE/ ACCEPTABLE SCRAP RATE/REJECTION COST/ REPAIR COSTS

These issues should never be discussed, some sellers will argue. "If I negotiate a rejection procedure, this tells the buyer my quality is not perfect." Professional negotiators should not take this position. If a rejection procedure is not clearly established before shipments start, the seller can be badly hurt if anything goes wrong. What will happen if the buyer refuses to pay, or ships the material back, or charges for repairs? The seller has three options: accept the buyer's action, go to court, or renegotiate. All three options are poor. Buyers and sellers are urged to discuss these points before signing the contract.

## TOLL MATERIAL

In some industries a buyer will buy raw materials from one company and send them to a second company for fabrication. This is called tolling material. If this applies, or could apply, the procedure must be worked out in great detail to protect your interests. A lawyer should be consulted by the buyer to assure that if the seller goes out of business the buyer can get the material. If this is not handled correctly the buyer may only get a percentage of the value.

## PERT CHARTS/FREQUENCY OF CHARTS/ MILESTONE SCHEDULE/DELIVERY SCHEDULE/ DELAY DELIVERY PROCEDURE

One of the biggest problems facing buyers is expediting. Checking vendors for delivery is an unpleasant chore. Buyers just do not like to do this. It is difficult and unpleasant work.

Smart buyers will ask for, or even demand, this information. This information should help reduce the buyer's expediting effort. The key to effective expediting is to prevent problems, not solve them. (E.g., fire prevention versus fire fighting.) The sooner a problem is uncovered, the easier it is to correct. The more control of production, the sooner problems are uncovered. A system that checks and monitors production effectively will increase the probability of on-time delivery.

Since this information is very valuable to the buyer, sellers can expect equal value in return. It certainly is to the seller's advantage to ship on time. This could be win-win for the seller.

## CONTAINER DEMURRAGE/CONTAINER DEPOSITS

In some industries a returnable container is used to deliver the material to the customer. Oxygen, nitrogen, and so forth are examples of such materials. The seller will take a position that the industry practice in regard to these items is that buyers pay. Buyers do not have to accept this; both issues are negotiable.

## KEY PERSONNEL/TECHNICAL HELP

Professional buyers will negotiate which of the seller's employees will work on the contract. This could have tremendous impact on the buyer's company.

In all groups of people, there is a range of performance. One person is the best, one person is the worst, and the others are ranked in between. This is relative, of course. The worst person may still do very acceptable work, or the best person may be marginal. It still is true that their performance can be ranked. As a buyer, I want the best customer service person working on my account, and I want the best engineer calling my factory. This point is negotiable and the buyer must try to get the best person available.

## LEASING OF EQUIPMENT OR MATERIAL/USING SPECIAL EQUIPMENT OR MATERIAL/LENDING OF EQUIPMENT/FREE ISSUE MATERIAL/LOANING OF MATERIAL

Sellers in particular should consider whether these areas offer any good possibilities for gain. The creative negotiator might be able to obtain a nice profit.

## ENGINEERING COSTS/DRAWING COSTS/WHO OWNS THE DRAWINGS/SOFTWARE COSTS/WHO OWNS THE SOFTWARE/SCOPE OF WORK/WHO HAS DESIGN RESPONSIBILITY

These issues are often not considered but are very important, especially for complex products.

## ENERGY

Today every buyer must be assured that his or her supplier has access to sufficient energy to complete the buyer's contract. During the first energy crisis, many companies could not ship at all or on time because they did not have enough natural gas, oil, electricity, and so forth.

## PLANT SUPPLIER WILL SHIP FROM

Some companies produce the same product at several plants. Buyers should keep quality records on a plant-by-plant basis. A general record for the supplier is not adequate. The buyer may find that one plant produces a higher quality product than the other plants. If so, the buyer should negotiate to have all of the material manufactured at the high-quality plant.

## MAINTENANCE MANUALS

It costs a lot of money to produce a complete maintenance manual. Sellers should not just give these away. They should receive an issue in the negotiation for agreeing to provide manuals.

## SAMPLES

Buyers should always expect free samples to test a potential supplier's product for engineering approval. This is true for all items purchased.

## POINT OR LOCATION OF DELIVERY

If the buyer has a large plant site with many unloading areas, the buyer should specify the exact delivery point. If not, the supplier may surprise the buyer with an extra bill for transportation.

## COMMISSION

If the seller receives a commission for each sale, this is a cost to the buyer and should be open to negotiation. A possible position is that a smaller commission is better than no commission.

## ERECTION RESPONSIBILITY/PERFORMANCE BOND/INSPECTION REQUIREMENTS/MATERIAL ASSURANCE OF SUPPLY/RETAINAGE

These items refer primarily to construction contracts (as do many other issues on this list). Retainage is very important for a buyer. It is normal for a buyer to pay progress payments (see Program Payments, Progress Payments, etc. subheading above), especially for major construction projects. Retainage is a percentage of each bill that is not paid, but retained until final completion. One of the best weapons that a buyer has to get the order completed is the money owed the supplier in the retaining account. The higher the retainage amount, the more power the buyer has.

## EMERGENCY PROCEDURES

A system should be set up to cover who to contact and how to contact them in case of emergencies. Who has the authorization to commit either side in an emergency should be clearly established long before the contract is signed or the order placed.

## REOPEN CLAUSE

Every good negotiator provides himself or herself many alternatives. The contract should contain a clause providing for renegotiation if conditions change. Of course, both sides should try to obtain one-way reopen clauses (i.e., only one party can initiate renegotiation).

## MAINTENANCE CONTRACTS

In the discussion of renewal parts, spare parts, and so forth the high profit margins that these items generate was mentioned. Maintenance contracts can produce the same type of profit. Buyers should be cautious in agreeing to a maintenance contract and should do so only after very careful consideration.

## MAKE OR BUY

Sellers usually are not prepared when the buyer says, "If you don't drop your price, we'll make it ourselves." The seller must know whether this really is a viable option or just a bluff. In many negotiations, this could be an important factor.

## APPROVED AUDITORS

If it is necessary to audit performance, costs, or any other part of the contract, the auditors should be established before the problem happens, not afterward.

## AUTHORIZATION FOR VENDOR INSPECTION TRIPS/ COST OF VENDOR AUDITS/TRAVEL COSTS

Buyers should take the position that an approval audit of a vendor's plant helps the vendor as much as it helps the buyer. The vendor stands to gain a lot of business if the vendor is approved, therefore, the vendor should expect to pay the cost of such audits.

## TYPE OF LABOR/TYPE OF MATERIAL

In checkpoint 11, cost analysis negotiation was discussed. During that procedure and any time a vendor is quoting labor or materials, these issues are important.

A vendor can make extra profit by using labor and/or materials that are of too high a quality for the job. This is especially true if general and administrative expenses and profit are determined as a percentage of direct costs. A vendor whose order book is nearly empty will want to retain the higher skilled labor, so the vendor may quote a job using these people instead of lower-skilled people who could do the work. Of course the other extreme is possible (workers are not qualified to do the work) and buyers must guard against this.

## OVERTIME—PREMIUM PAYMENTS

The cost of overtime is frequently misunderstood. In the direct product cost in the following example, the vendor has included the cost of labor at the normal hourly rate.

| | |
|---|---|
| Direct material | $100 |
| Direct labor | |
| (10 hours @ $5.00 per hour) | 50 |
| Direct costs | $150 |
| G + A (10% of costs) | 15 |
| | $165 |
| Profit (10%) | 17 |
| Selling price | $182 |

If this vendor works overtime to produce this item, the vendor will sell the items manufactured on overtime at a price of $182.00 each. This includes all direct labor at the normal rate. The vendor must pay direct labor $7.50 per hour ($5.00 plus $1/2$ for each hour of overtime). Since $5.00 per hour of this is already included in the $182, the buyer should only accept an overtime premium of $2.50 per hour, or a total of $25.00 in this example. The buyer should also negotiate the two 10 percent adders (G + A and profit). A buyer can make a strong case that no additional G + A expense is incurred by the seller.

Profit is wide open for negotiation. This point is one that should be settled before the final deal. Buyers can save their principals significant sums in this area.

## VENDOR'S LABOR CONTRACTS/SUBTIER LABOR CONTRACTS/UNION LABOR REQUIRED OR NOT REQUIRED

A smart buyer will discuss these three points in considerable depth. In the final contract they may not seem important. However, if a problem occurs during the life of the contract it could cost more than the value of the original contract.

## ADVANTAGES FOR OTHER LOCATIONS

Any individual who works for a multiplant or multilocation company should consider the other locations during negotiations. It is possible that a buyer may be able to negotiate corporate volume instead of one-location volume and receive a better deal. A seller may be able to package a total volume deal and get more sales.

## KANBAN/SHORT-CYCLE DELIVERY

This inventory concept that is used in Japan is based upon a very short lead time (hours or days) and close cooperation between buyers and sellers. A significant amount of openness must be established before this point can be negotiated, since both sides will assume significant responsibility in the final contract.

## BUYER'S EDUCATION

Generally the seller knows more about the product than the buyer does. A smart seller may want to negotiate this point. Every industry and each business in that industry has special individual needs.

## ADDITIONAL POINTS

The following additional points are listed to remind the negotiator during the planning of a negotiation that they may need to be investigated. Again, it cannot be emphasized too much that if one side is prepared to negotiate a point and the other side is not prepared, the prepared side usually wins the point.

Insurance
Taxes
Standards
Options
Purchase specifications
Equal-to-brands
Special codes and standards
Trade-in value
Legal points
Boiler plate (information on back of purchase order)
Start-up help/costs
Current value of money
Extra charges
Storage costs
Inspection requirements
Overtime rates
U.S. Laws
Advertisements
Publicity
Endorsements (buyer for the seller)
Restocking procedure
Special environment requirements
Special customer service needs
Who will be third party (arbitrators)
Appeal procedure
Resale/repurchase agreements
Safety
Pollution

Installation costs

Special deals/charges and so forth

Field service

I'm sure that I have missed several issues. It is suggested that you review this list and write in the issues that should be considered for your company's special needs. Here are a few spaces for the reader to add these issues:

1. _____
2. _____
3. _____
4. _____
5. _____
6. _____
7. _____
8. _____
9. _____
10. _____

Finally, do not forget that the product to be negotiated has many factors that lend themselves to negotiation. Such items as size, weight, chemistry, and so forth must be considered in the planning of a buyer-seller negotiation.

# CHAPTER 6

# Management-Labor Issues to Be Negotiated

Buyers and sellers almost always think of price first. For labor and management, the first issue is wages (the price of labor). Listed are numerous issues that must be considered during the planning stage of every management-labor negotiation. These issues cover most business situations. However, each management-labor negotiation is unique, and the negotiator should add to the list any additional points for the particular negotiation being planned.

Wages are listed first, but it is not the only issue and may not be the most significant issue, in terms of the total cost versus total benefits in the package. Although some of the issues have been grouped, they must each be considered as individual issues to be negotiated.

## WAGES

This issue covers the actual cost of labor to management. It will be expressed as a rate/time period (e.g., $6.09/hour, $574/week, $2,700/month). The major point of the negotiation is the amount of increase or decrease. This can be stated as an absolute ($.57/hour) or a percentage. An absolute increase allows workers at all levels to receive the same raise. However, the more skilled workers at the higher pay scales will receive smaller percentage raises. For example, $.57/hour is 10 percent of the $5.70/hour rate but only five percent of an $11.40/hour rate. With an absolute raise, the less skilled, younger people receive more (on a percentage basis).

For years wages only went up. The only point to be negotiated was how much. In the United States this changed in the early 1980s. Many contracts were negotiated with "give-backs" of lower wages and/or benefits. Now it is not a given that wages must go up. It is negotiable. A percentage raise gives equal treatment to all workers at any point in time. There is a problem over time. The difference between wage levels will not remain constant. This example will prove this point:

|  | Labor Grade #1 | Labor Grade #9 | Difference |
|---|---|---|---|
| Start | $2.00/hr | $5.00/hr | $3.00 |
| 10% raise | .20 | .50 | |
| New pay | $2.20 | $5.50 | $3.30 |
| 10% raise | .22 | .55 | |
| New pay | $2.42 | $6.05 | $3.63 |
| 10% raise | .24 | .61 | |
| New pay | $2.66 | $6.66 | $4.00 |

After three 10% raises, the difference between the two labor grades went up $33^{1}/_{2}$% because of compounding.

From the labor standpoint the question as to which type of raise is best is often answered by the age distribution of the work force. Because this point is the easiest to understand and has the highest visibility, it gets the most pressure. The worker can see the results of a big raise, but cannot see the results as clearly for many of the other issues. The other issues provide the worker with significant advantages, but are much harder for the worker to understand. Because of this, much pressure will be felt by both sides on wages.

The professional negotiator knows that wages must be treated with special care, but the negotiator must not concentrate too much on wages and too little on other issues. The management negotiator also knows that in almost every case the increases given to labor will also be given to all others in the company. (This is most important for product cost considerations.)

## SKILLED LABOR PREMIUMS

In many labor negotiations skilled labor premiums will become important. In addition to the raise that all workers receive, the skilled labor grades will receive another raise. The major reason is the belief that these unique skills should not be hurt because an absolute raise is granted by management. To offset the effects of an absolute raise, labor should demand a skilled labor extra.

## SKILLED LABOR GRADES

If there is an extra for the higher labor grades, another issue to be negotiated is what labor grades are really skilled. Labor should try to cover as many grades as possible. Since the premium becomes part of the base grade, management must be very careful. All future product costs will be affected by the agreement in this area. Also to be considered by management is the future ripple effect. This year labor may have a few labor grades designated as skilled labor grades. For the next negotiation, labor will try to get others added, with the objective of having all grades eventually getting a skill labor premium. Then labor can start again at the top.

A standard labor strategy should be to ask for one premium to be paid to the top half of the labor grades and less to the other grades, and then back off to a sliding scale. Here is an example of a skilled labor premium pay scale:

| Labor Grade | Skilled Extra |
|:-----------:|:-------------:|
| 16 | $.50/hour |
| 15 | $.50/hour |
| 14 | $.50/hour |
| 13 | $.30/hour |
| 12 | $.30/hour |
| 11 | $.30/hour |
| 10 | $.20/hour |
| 9 | $.20/hour |
| 1–8 | Nothing |

## DAY WORK PAY/MEASURED DAY WORK PAY/ PIECE RATE PAY/PIECE RATE MAKEUP PAY/PIECE RATE ONLY ON GOOD PIECES/BASE PAY PLUS COMMISSION/BASE PAY PLUS A DRAW

Pay rates can have a major impact on costs, management styles, and the work environment. First, consider day work. For labor this is a "guaranteed" pay. For example, if the rate is $11.30/hour and a worker is on the job eight hours, the worker will receive gross pay of $90.40. If the worker produced 10 parts, 100 parts, or 500 parts, the worker gets the same pay. For management, the more parts it can get labor to produce in eight hours, the lower the unit cost will be. A style of management that produces maximum effort will produce low cost. Many times management will set a standard for production and this is known as "measured day work."

Second, consider piece rate pay. For management this is a guaranteed cost per unit. For example, the rate might be $.50 per unit, so there is a fixed labor cost for all items of $.50. For employees, pay is variable based upon how hard they work. Another consideration for labor is what happens if a necessary machine is not operating and labor cannot produce. This is where makeup pay is so important. That is the pay that management gives to workers, when through no fault of their own, they cannot produce.

The following examples will show the impact these points can have:

Assume a labor rate of $12.00/hour. Assume a standard of 48 units/hour.

Labor will make $96.00/day. Management has a labor cost per unit of $.25.

If management can get labor to produce 60 units/hour, labor will make $96.00/day, and management has a labor cost per unit of $.20. (This is a 20 percent improvement from standard.)

If labor will only produce 30 units/hour, labor will make $96.00/day, and management has a labor cost per unit of $.40. (This is a 60 percent decrease from standard.)

Now assume a piece rate of $.13/unit. Management has a labor cost per unit of $.13. Labor has no guarantee of pay. It is only based upon actual production.

Finally, from the management standpoint, if a piece rate pay schedule is in effect, management should only pay for parts that pass inspection. The counting point must be after inspection, not before. The cost per unit could vary greatly if all parts are paid for rather than just acceptable parts.

## SECTION INCENTIVE PAY/OFF-SHIFT INCENTIVE PAY/SECOND-SHIFT BONUS/THIRD-SHIFT BONUS/ OVERTIME PAY RULES

Piece rate pay can also be paid on a section or shift basis. Under these systems of pay, all those in a particular group will be paid based upon the production of the total group. There are strong pluses and minuses for these types of systems. If you are negotiating such a system you must be sure that the ground rules are simple, clear, and easy to control.

For many years people working on a shift other than the normal daytime period (i.e., 7:00 A.M. to 3:30 P.M., 8:00 A.M. to 4:30 P.M., 9:00 A.M. to 5:00 P.M.) have been paid a bonus. Second shift (3:00 P.M.

to 11:00 P.M.) traditionally gets 5–15 percent extra and third shift (11:00 P.M. to 7:00 A.M.) gets 10–20 percent extra. However a new labor contract starts from zero, so these matters can be negotiated each time. This was especially true on management's part during the early 1980s.

There are labor laws that govern overtime pay rules—how much should be paid for more than eight hours per day for work, more than 40 hours in a week, for Sunday and holiday work, and so forth. This does not mean that labor cannot negotiate for more than the legal minimum. A tactic that management might use is, "We are obeying the law." Labor should counter that the law only sets the base. Labor can use the example of the minimum wage laws. Many workers in the United States are governed by minimum wage laws, but are paid significantly above the minimum wage level.

## COST OF LIVING

Cost-of-living index

Cost-of-living base

Cost-of-living adjustment dates

Cost-of-living percentage

Cost-of-living review period

Cost-of-living added to base

As the inflation rate has sharply increased in the United States, cost-of-living (COL) issues have become very important. In order for employees to "maintain their current standard of living," a cost-of-living clause should be negotiated. Five factors must be considered: first, the index that will be used to measure inflation. Second, the base that will be used as the starting point to measure inflation. The impact of these two will be very significant. Next, when adjustments will be made (by month, by quarter, by half, by year, etc.) and when the new wage rate will be reflected in the wages paid. A fourth point will take much planning work and negotiation effort—what the percentage will be. If the inflation index (usually the Consumer Price Index) goes up by one percent, what will be the raise for labor? Success or failure on this issue could determine the success or failure of the negotiator. Both sides must do a lot of planning on this point. They must construct economic models for the future, and the best model may determine which side wins this point.

The last factor to be considered is when the cost-of-living adjustment gets added to the base pay grades. The labor position is that this should be immediately put into the base. Because it can be a significant cost to management, management should resist. Management should strive for base pay and COL pay to be separate. This way COL can be negotiated at each negotiation. Once it is in the base pay, it really is no longer a negotiation issue.

## LENGTH OF CONTRACT/EXPIRATION DATE/ CONTRACT START DATE

Since each contract is new, the length of it and therefore the expiration date must be negotiated. Checkpoint 1 discussed time issues in a buyer-seller context. The same considerations that the buyer made should be made by labor and management. Another factor, however, enters for management-labor negotiation—strikes. If a strike is necessary, the negotiator should consider the best time for one from his or her principal's standpoint.

In the automobile industry for example, it might be best for labor to have the contract end at the high point of the sales year. This would put extra pressure on management. Management could lose a lot of sales if there is a strike. Perhaps management will "pay" a little more to have no strike and full production and high sales. December might also be a good time for a potential strike. It could be suggested that management might look very bad if their workers were on strike in December (no Christmas or Hanukkah presents, walking the picket line in subzero temperatures, etc.) rather than in May.

The negotiator must take into consideration when the best time for the next negotiation will be. It might be best to give on other issues to get this issue in the negotiator's favor.

The longer the contract, the more risk for both sides, especially if all the financial points are firm. The longer the contract, the better for management because they are "assured" of continued production. Management can make all their strategic plans, because they know production will not stop. Labor has a stronger assurance of continued work. If conditions change significantly, one side will be hurt.

There is a tendency to continue past practice with regard to contract length. If the two sides have always had three-year contracts, then the current negotiation is assumed to be for three years. This is an undesirable attitude, however, for each negotiation is different and separate. If one side allows the other to win the issue on length of contract, then that side should expect something in return. In hundreds of case studies I have seen one side give in on an issue and get nothing in return. This should not happen. If your side allows the other to have an issue, your side should get something in return. This is especially true in management-labor negotiations. The length of the contract is a perfect example. If management wants a three-year contract (to assure stable production), then labor should get something in return. If labor wants a one-year contract (to be able to try to get more next year), then management should get something in return.

If there is a strike, the length of the new contract can start from two dates: the date the last contract expired or the date the new contract is signed. This is another issue to be negotiated.

## MEDICAL BENEFITS ISSUES

Surgery costs

Hospital costs

Dental costs

Eye doctor costs

Office visit costs

Major medical costs and percentage

Diagnostic costs

Laboratory costs

X-ray tests

Medicine and drugs

Therapy

Rehabilitation

Psychiatric costs

Hospital "special services"

Maternity costs

Alcohol programs

Drug programs

Annual physical exams

Remote location complete physical exams

The subject of medical benefits could be covered in a separate book. Today these costs are so high (a semiprivate hospital room could cost $300–$600/day) that medical benefits are a significant cost to management and benefit to labor. It is not possible to cover all the details of medical benefits here. The negotiator must do a lot of planning and get all the facts. Both sides must consider the actual costs and then look at the specific labor force in question. A small error could cost millions of dollars in the future.

## SICK LEAVE PAYMENTS/DISABILITY PAYMENTS/ ACCIDENT PAYMENTS/MATERNITY LEAVE

How much time off the job will be allowed because of medical problems and how much (if any) pay the worker will get can pose significant large costs to management. The rules for these benefits must be negotiated. As with many subjects of management-labor negotiations, these issues require much data and planning. It is not possible to negotiate these issues without the facts. The cost to business in the United States each year and the resultant benefit to labor is tremendous.

## INSURANCE BENEFITS

Life insurance

Accident and dismemberment insurance

Life insurance for spouse

Accident insurance for spouse

Life insurance for children

Accident insurance for children

Travel insurance

Insurance benefits are similar to the medical benefits subject. It is impossible to cover all of the details in this book. The issues are listed here to assure that management-labor negotiators remember to plan for them before each negotiation.

Because these issues involve future costs and benefits, and because these are not completely predictable, much planning will be required. A detailed analysis of past payouts is necessary as a base. Then the negotiator should project future payments under three conditions—the worst possible conditions, the best possible conditions, and the most probable conditions.

Again, it should not be forgotten that any small mistake could result in millions of dollars during the life of the contract (and possibly future contracts).

## OTHER BENEFITS ISSUES

Legal assistance

Legal assistance for family members

Credit union

Stock plan

Bonus

On-the-job training

Educational assistance

Christmas bonus

Company support of employee activities

Purchase of company products

Purchase of subsidiary products

After-hours off-the-job training

During-working-hours off-the-job training

Industrial training programs in another organization

In-company college courses

Many of these other benfits are training benefits. Today training is a most important part of our industrial/commercial world. Almost every employee requires structured on-the-job training, from the janitor to middle management. A growing percentage of training funds are being devoted to many types of training. This is particularly true of off-the-job, formal training courses during working hours. For many years top management, middle management, supervisory, and professional employees have participated in these types of courses. Today all employees at many companies are participating in training and many are requesting courses. Examples of courses include: "Management Techniques." "Management Grid," "Management By Objective," "Business Management," "Fundamentals of Purchasing," "Basic Sales Techniques," "Directing the Engineering Project."

Mr. Alvin Toffler is the author of two books, *Future Shock* and *The Third Wave*, that discuss our rapidly changing society, and indicates that learning and retaining new skills will become more and more important in all future management-labor negotiations. Another book, *Megatrends*, by John Naisbitt, addresses the 10 most important trends in our society in the 1980s. All of these books would be helpful reading for anyone involved in labor-management negotiations.

Most companies today offer educational assistance programs in the form of paying employees' college tuition costs or providing college courses at company locations. In very few cases are all costs covered. Labor should take the position that all costs (books, travel, supplies, etc.) should be paid.

## SAVINGS PLANS (COMPANY CONTRIBUTION, HOLDING PERIOD, INVESTMENT OPPORTUNITIES, EMERGENCY WITHDRAWAL PRIVILEGES)

Savings plans are very widespread. In general, the subject of negotiation will be how much an employee can contribute, what the holding period will be, where will the money be invested, and how much the company will contribute. If no plan exists, this could be a major issue to be negotiated.

## RECREATION FACILITIES/ALLOWED ACTIVITIES DURING WORK

The subject of recreation facilities has many aspects. As our society becomes more aware of the positive aspects of good physical condition and the need to relieve stress, this negotiation issue will increase in importance. A number of companies have workout rooms (some with trained specialists), tracks, and so forth. There is a wide range of possible agreements concerning recreational facilities and activities. One major corporation, for example, allows families to use its recreation facilities during the weekend.

## PENSION ISSUES

Preretirement training programs

Noncontributory pension

Contributory pension

Vesting rights time period

Minimum time to receive full pension

Minimum age to receive full pension

Early retirement bonus

Early retirement guidelines

Survivor rights

Pension increases for retirees

Long-term disability

Company-sponsored IRA

Company participation in IRA contributions

Company handling paperwork for IRA

Company including spouse in IRA matters

Pension issues are critical in any management-labor negotiation. In the 1980s it might be the second most critical in the United States. Inflation in the 1970s destroyed the concept that a good pension at age 65 would be a good pension at age 85. The average payout in one major company is 180 pension checks, or 15 years. With just an eight percent rate of inflation and no change in pension payments, the re-tirees' standard of living at the end of 15 years will be less than half what it was at the beginning. With medical advances young people today can expect to receive more than 180 pension checks. Adjust-ments to pensions for current retirees is a cost to the company but may not be perceived as a benefit to labor's negotiators. This is an excellent example of a potential difference between the needs of the negotiator and the needs of the principal. Each labor negotiator must remember that he or she will be retired some day. Another example of a conflict of needs would be if management's chief negotiator is very close to retirement. In such a case, the negotiator's needs might be very different from the company's needs.

How much does an employee have to contribute and how much benefit the employee gains is important. Here the value of current money versus the value of future money is a key question. What other uses can be made for that current money might determine ne-gotiating positions.

"Vesting rights time period" simply means how long an employee has to work for a company before the pension earned will be paid, even if the employee leaves. For example, if an employee works 10 years at a major corporation, the employee is entitled to a pension at age 62 or 65. The amount of the pension will only be equal to 10 times the value of one year's service. The important idea is that a pen-sion is paid. Laws may affect this point but, as stated earlier, labor can ask for more than the law requires.

Since 1981 individual workers are entitled to have an Individual Retirement Account (IRA). Labor will be taking the position that management should handle the paperwork and transfer funds as di-rected by the individual. Management should develop the costs of this benefit and, if it is agreed to, ask for equal value from labor on another issue.

Since the value of these issues is in the future and cannot be pre-cisely determined, a lot of work is necessary when planning the ne-gotiation of each of these points.

## JOB SECURITY

Lifetime employment

Unemployment benefits

Layoff procedure

Firing procedure

Relocating displaced employees

Retraining displaced employees

Job security may be the most critical subject of management-labor negotiations in the 1980s. The size and shape of the labor force in the United States is rapidly changing. Thousands of jobs are being eliminated forever. How will these people be treated? That is a key issue. Both management and labor will have these several job security points high on their priority lists.

It would probably be wise to negotiate all of these job security issues at the same time. Because they are interrelated, it is likely to be difficult to negotiate these issues at different times in the negotiation process.

## PRODUCTIVITY

Another critical area in the 1980s is productivity. How much output is expected from each employee? How will this be determined? How will this be measured? Several books have been written on this subject. Every labor-management negotiator should take advantage of the extended treatment of this issue in these books.

## TIME-OFF BENEFITS ISSUES

Vacation

Holidays

Personal days

Death in family

Sick leave

Leave of absence (education, personal, medical)

Jury duty

Military duty

Seniority for each time-off benefit

Any day that an employee gets paid for but does not work is a major benefit to the employee and a major cost to the company. In many large manufacturing companies a 30-year employee is entitled to 48 days off per year with pay (30 days vacation, 12 holidays, and six personal days). Each year has 261 working days (365 days less 104 weekend days). A 30-year employee in that company only has to work about 81 percent of the total working days to get a full year's pay. For every five such employees, the company will have to hire a sixth worker.

Two important points to remember: First, each contract is new, so management can take the position that the new contract will have less paid time. This is a very negotiable issue. Second, all workers do not have to have the same benefits. Seniority can be the distinguishing factor, for example.

## WORK AREA ISSUES

Seniority

Upgrade procedures

Job blending

Job sharing

Line of progression

Guaranteed pay if overtime is worked

Amount of overtime

Job qualification

Super seniority

Increase/decrease

Normal workweek

Normal work hours

Equalization of overtime

Breaks

Wash-up time

Flextime

Procedure to rerate jobs

Procedure to grade new jobs

Bulletin board

Job posting

Down-time rules

Tip sharing

Uniforms

Dress code

Dress code—off-hours work

Parking

Location of time clocks

Company cafeteria

Work-out of job classification

These issues fall into the general category of work area points to be negotiated. Most do not need any discussion and only a few need a description.

Job blending refers to expanding a job to include parts of other jobs. This is intended to make each job more interesting. Job sharing refers to two or more people working at one job, each part-time. For example, two people may share a secretarial job. One person works Monday, Tuesday, and Wednesday; the second person works Thursday and Friday. If job sharing is adopted, both sides must agree on how pensions, vacations, seniority, and so forth will affect the people sharing a job. Many such potential problems should be anticipated during the negotiation.

Line of progression refers to "families of jobs." In many plants certain jobs naturally follow other jobs. In the maintenance area it might be (1) oiler, (2) general helper, (3) machine setup, (4) machine repair, and (5) senior maintenance. Employees in the line of progression would receive preference for open jobs in their area.

Equalization of overtime means that all employees must have equal opportunity to work overtime. Their supervisor must keep track of all overtime worked and any overtime refused. (Refused overtime is considered worked for purposes of equalizing overtime opportunity.) The total for all employees over a certain time period (generally three months) must be the same.

Flextime is a newer concept that allows employees to determine what hours they will work. Currently most flextime arrangements are in office environments. A typical flextime company would have these rules:

1.  All employees must be in the office between 9:00 A.M. and 3:00 P.M. (unless of course they are traveling on business). This is "core time."
2.  All employees must take at least 30 minutes for lunch during core time.
3.  The balance of the day must be worked between 7:00 A.M. and 7:00 P.M.
4.  A total of 40 hours must be worked each week.

The control of flextime can be very costly and/or very difficult. The benefits to the worker are tremendous.

## SAFETY AND SAFETY EQUIPMENT

The use of safety equipment should not be open to question. However, it must be. Thousands of people have been injured or killed because of the lack of safety equipment, improper safety equipment, or refusal to use safety equipment.

Safe working conditions is another issue. Most people believe that a safe working environment should never be a question. But even in the 1980s it is. As with many issues, this can become a very emotional issue. Negotiations should do everything possible to keep the negotiations on this issue positive and objective.

## PROBLEM RESOLUTION ISSUES

Grievance procedure

Arbitration

Mediation

Open door to top management

How will problems between management and labor be handled? These four issues will set the rules. The key item for arbitration and mediation is the selection of the outside person to arbitrate or mediate any disputes. Many times who this person will be is more important than the facts, because the person's background and/or bias will greatly influence the decision.

## MANAGEMENT AUTHORITY ISSUES

Subcontract rights

Purchased parts rights

Technology improvements

Robotics

Plant rules

Discipline

Supervisors' right to return to labor jobs

Attendance rules

Right to move employees

Right to hire temporary employees

Position descriptions

Work flow

Profit sharing

Suggestion system

Quality circle programs

Most people would agree that these matters listed fall under management's authority. That is, management can make decisions in these areas without consulting labor. This does not mean that labor should not try to negotiate these issues. Labor has nothing to lose if it tries to gain concessions from management. In some agreements, some of these issues have been included. Management negotiators must be prepared for each of these issues.

## UNION AUTHORITY ISSUES

Costs of union meetings

Time off for union meetings

Size of negotiating team

Union meeting place

In-plant sales

Special treatment for union officials

Checkoff for union dues

Time off for grievance meetings

Time off for union training

These nine items, most would agree, fall within labor's authority and/or rights. As with the management authority points discussed previously, these are very negotiable and labor must be prepared to negotiate.

## NEW PLANT/CLOSE PLANT ISSUES

Ability to move to a new plant

Notification requirements

Notification period

Relocation of employees

Relocation costs

Retraining of employees not moved

Payment for out placement seminars

Company "neutral" at new plant

Employees purchase plant options

Issues concerning closing plants and opening new ones have become very important as industrial production has declined in the United States and as many companies have moved to the Sunbelt. Labor has a lot to lose if it does not do a good negotiating job on these issues.

## INFORMATION GIVEN TO OPPONENTS/COST TO PREPARE INFORMATION

How much information one side can demand be given to it by the other side is an important point to be negotiated. Labor should always ask for every conceivable piece of information in order not to disclose beforehand what points it regards as the most important. Management will generally not want to give this information to labor. If it does, the cost of collecting the information is an issue to be considered for negotiation.

## TRAVEL BENEFITS ISSUES

Mileage for use of personal car

Airline tickets (first versus coach)

Motels (first class versus standard)

Meals

Ground transportation

Per-diem allowance

Authorization for family accompanying employee on business trip

Family paid for on business trip

Use of company cars

Use of company airplanes

Maximum amount of travel

Whenever an employee travels for the company, significant expenses will be incurred. Management generally has the right to make all decisions in all of these areas. Again labor could try to negotiate these issues, so management must be prepared.

## OTHER ISSUES

Van pool/car pool plans

Portal-to-portal pay

Free coffee at coffee breaks

Equal employment opportunities/affirmative action

Use of minority vendors

Use of small business vendors

Buy America only

Buy union made material only

Sponsorship of athletic teams

Family gratuities

Stock options

Company matching donations to higher education

Company matching donations to civic organizations

Company matching donations to charitable organizations

United fund

Service awards

Membership in professional/trade organizations—authorization

Costs of membership in professional/trade organizations

Exchange programs—government

Exchange programs—nonprofit organizations

"Loaned" employee programs (United Fund, etc.)

These "other issues" have been discussed at one time or another in management-labor negotiations. They may not always be high on the priority lists but they should be considered because of the potential costs and benefits in the final agreement.

## AGREEMENT ALTERATION ISSUES

Renegotiation

Reopen clauses

Modify

Terminate

Before a final agreement can be reached between management and labor, issues concerning the alteration of the agreement must also be negotiated. Again, the considerations in Chapter 4 apply here.

Here are a few spaces for the reader to jot down the issues that rapidly come to mind for the reader's unique situation.

1. _____
2. _____
3. _____
4. _____
5. _____
6. _____
7. _____
8. _____
9. _____
10. _____

# CHAPTER 7

# Business-Business Issues to Be Negotiated

There are several types of negotiations that can be defined as business-business negotiations: Company A wants to merge with Company B, Company A and Company B are considering a joint venture, Company A wants to buy out Company B, and so forth. These can be very complex. A considerable amount of fact-finding will be necessary. Each negotiation will be very specialized and the following issues listed will represent only a small percentage of the total issues. They are listed by the six major functional areas in business—human resources, manufacturing, purchasing, engineering, marketing, and finance. The nature of the negotiation will establish whether the item is important during fact-finding (i.e., determining level of performance) or negotiations (i.e., determining value of area).

## HUMAN RESOURCES

### Employment

Determining need for individual
Requisition
Recruiting
Interviewing
Testing
Job Offer
Orientation
Counseling

### Upgrading Employees

Performance management systems
Assessment centers
Seniority systems

### Termination

Step process
Review and counseling
Exit interviews

### Training

Needs analysis procedure
Total development system
Instructor training system
Percentage of training versus education
On-the-job training
Apprenticeship
Technical training

Professional training
Supervisory training
Management training
Conferences
Functional meetings
Library
Programmed instructions
Tuition assistance programs

## Compensation

Job descriptions
Job standards
Wage scales (including cost of living)
Wage ranges (including area wage scales)
Incentives
Bonuses
Performance review system
Top Management Program
Profit sharing

## Safety and Security

Procedures
Enforcement system
Inspections
Education
OSHA Reviews
Investigations
Hazardous materials
Physical examination procedures
First aid training

## Working Conditions

Space per employee
Lighting
Ventilation
Heating and cooling
Noise
Toxic fumes
Exposure problems
Breaks
Lunch room facilities
Parking facilities
Accident investigations and records

## Contractual Considerations

All the items listed in Chapter 6 should be considered.

## MANUFACTURING

## Production Control

Long-term forecasting
Short-term forecasting
Short-term scheduling
Economical lot size
Feeder scheduling
Subassembly scheduling
Final assembly scheduling
Machine loading system
Manpower system
Work-in-process control
Bottleneck identification

Total manufacturing cycle
Overtime planned and unplanned
Make-or-buy decisions

## Inventory Control

Reporting system
Control of material movement
Requisition initiation system
Requisition authorization system
Safety stock/inventory level
Material requirements planning
Order review point
Economical ordering quantities
Storage of raw materials
Storage of purchased parts
Storage of work in process
Storage of finished stock
Material handling equipment
Access to storerooms
Storeroom requisition procedure
Large, medium, small item analysis
Standardization

## Line Operations

Scheduling of personnel
Scheduling of individual machines
Allowable overruns
On-the-job training system
Overtime assignments and equalization
Productivity measurements
Productivity improvement programs

Absenteeism rates
Turnover rates
Employee bumping system

## Quality Control

Receiving inspection controls
First-piece inspections
Subassembly inspections
Final-assembly inspections
Patrol inspections
Defective material review procedures
Use of substandard material
Quality improvement system

## Maintenance

Method of record keeping
Technical information system
Routine maintenance policy
Routine maintenance system and schedules
Vacation shutdown maintenance system
Emergency system
Work-order procedure
Replacement parts inventory and reordering
Control of tools and equipment

## Manufacturing/Industrial Engineering

Scheduling and assignments
Capital programs versus day-to-day needs
Time-study procedures
Capital appropriations procedures
Return on investment analysis system

## Purchasing

Centralized versus decentralized

Vendor rating system

Blanket order system

Buying assignment procedures

Completeness of specification file

Completeness of vendor files

Requisition review procedure

Quotation request/analysis procedure

Vendor selection procedure

Negotiation requirements and procedures

Paperwork procedures

Cost analysis/value analysis/price analysis

Long-term contracts versus order-by-order purchasing

Sale-of-scrap procedures

Expediting system

Number of sole source items

## Research and development

Quality and quantity of personnel

Scope of research

Library and technical information

Percentage of gross sales billed for innovation

Percentage of gross sales billed for product modification

Research concepts

How go/no-go decisions are made

Scope of pilot testing programs

Interface with line operations

Number of patents, copyrights, and so forth

Interface with universities

## Product Engineering

Engineering policies and company goals

Interface with marketing/customers

Project scheduling procedures

Work plans

Budget/schedule controls

Measurement of engineering performance

Standard cost development procedures

Use of computer aided engineering system

## MARKETING

### Market Research

Process to determine customer needs

Economic trend analysis techniques

Geographic market information

Forecasting procedures

Forecasting accuracy

Potential customer profiles

Market boundary data

Product/market comparison files

Use of consultants' information

Use of government information

Annual reports of customer files

### Pricing

Absorption versus direct costing system

Break-even analysis

Type of contracts

Market information feedback system

Competitive information feedback system

Price changes system

Price improvement system/evaluation

### Advertising

Number of trade shows attended

Association meetings attended

Advertising effectiveness indicators

Product information materials

Direct/indirect market information

Priorities by product

Percentage of gross sales billed

Catalog preparation

### Sales

Customer information files

Customer requirements files

Sales call rates

Ratio of calls to actual sales

Cost of sales calls

Product mix analysis

Variance of actual sales to forecasts

Bonus/incentive systems

Feedback (engineering, research, etc.) system

Product training system

Interpersonal training system

Proposal preparation system

Negotiation planning procedures

Sales area guidelines

Profit margin versus sales efforts

Lost sales analysis procedures

## Customer Service

System to follow customer due dates
Internal expediting system
Inventory status system
Distribution channels

## FINANCE

## Planning

Top-management information system
Strategic planning versus short-term gains
Prebudget review system
Forecasts—schedules and accuracy
Timeliness of information

## Computers and Data Processing

Security of information
Feasibility study process
Equipment selection process
User interface before purchase
Long-term/short-term decision process
Cost effectiveness of data processing
System analysis procedures
User group feedback system
Programming costs versus system effectiveness
Control of priorities for work assignments
Management involvement
System design
Input methods and accuracy checks
Personal computer usage

User training
Format of output information
Data maintenance system

## Accounting

Accounts payable system

Accounts receivable system

Cash-flow management

Timeliness-of-operations information

Management-by-exception reports

Independent auditor interface

Cost management system

These issues cover the six functional areas found in most business. They will not all apply to every negotiation, but they must be considered and modified for each specific negotiation.

The last area to consider is management. This covers a very broad area and is intended to stimulate more issues for possible negotiation. Management reaches all areas and units in a company and its quality determines the organization's effectiveness. Top management is accountable for the continued growth of the company.

## MANAGEMENT

Quality of personnel

Policy decision-making process

Corporate culture

Resource development

Corporate strategic planning activities

Corporate objectives

Use of functions of management

Planning

Organizing

Implementing

Controlling

Finally, before the negotiation, all finanical records must be reviewed in detail to assure that no surprises occur after the negotiation.

Some of these items will be significant for getting information about the other company. The negotiator or fact finder must delve into the details from two perspectives: (1) the management system (planning, organization, delegation, communication, and control); and (2) the information (how, what, why, when, where, and who). The negotiator must also be alert to other issues that may be uncovered.

The issues investigated may not be actually negotiated, but the information will be most important beause it will help evaluate the other company and will be important when placing a total value on the other company. The information will also help assess the amount of investment that is necessary to bring any substandard area or item up to an acceptable lead. When a person buys a second-hand car, the person must determine how much it will cost, after the purchase, to get the car into first-class running condition. The same is true when one company buys another or a merger is considered.

# CHAPTER 8

# Meetings and Conference Issues to Be Negotiated

Another type of negotiation that many businesspeople participate in is the negotiation to set up a business meeting, a training course, a trade show, a conference, and so forth. This usually involves a motel, hotel, or conference center (seller) and the meeting manager (buyer).

Many of the issues covered in Chapters 5 and 6 are important and should be reviewed. Discussed here are additional issues that should be considered. The priority will, of course, depend upon the particular negotiation.

## TIME MEETING ROOM IS AVAILABLE

Many meetings are scheduled at large properties. It is possible that another meeting will be held just before yours in the same room. If your meeting has an extensive setup—rear screen projection, booths, display areas, and so forth, this issue could be very critical. The property management will want a fast turnover. Nonproductive space is lost revenue. Another major issue for day meetings is whether your setup will be torn down at night for another group and then reset in the morning. If so, the meeting manager should ask for a discount and an assurance of a perfect reset each day.

## HOW MUCH SETUP CAN YOUR COMPANY DO ITSELF?

Many companies have experts who can set up a meeting. However, some properties have exclusive contracts that all such labor must be done by local people. This is still a negotiable issue, especially if the setup is technical in nature.

## SETUP CONFIDENTIALITY

Many meetings' purpose is to announce a new product or idea. The meeting manager must get absolute guarantees that no information will be leaked by employees of the hotel.

## LABOR AVAILABILITY

The meeting manager should have a written commitment from the property manager that the required amount and correct type of labor (e.g., electricians, carpenters, movers, etc.) will be available for the meeting. Many meeting managers mistakenly assume that overtime will solve any possible problems. This is not a good position and should never be taken. Proper planning and a good negotiation should eliminate the need for overtime.

## LABOR RATES

What the rates are for straight time and for overtime is important. A rate schedule, including all trades and experience levels, should be part of all contracts.

## LABOR HOURS

What the normal straight-time hours are must be determined. Is there a night shift whose pay differential is only 10 percent? If so, that will save a large amount of money as compared with overtime. Also to be determined is what hours are overtime hours and what hours are double time hours. Are Saturdays, Sundays, and holidays under special pay rules? Are workers guaranteed a minimum number of hours per day, per job, and so forth? All these questions must be negotiated and agreed to in writing before any meeting contract is finalized.

## ROOM SETUP CHARGES

Room setup charges are very negotiable. One formula is cost per task (i.e., $.57 to set up or take down a chair). Another formula is cost per hour. Several possible formulas should be considered. The layout should be reviewed. A simple layout with a core that is usable for all parts of the meeting will save considerably. Minor changes made around the core can accommodate various needs during the sessions. A floor plan must be part of the final contract.

## UTILITY CHARGES

Utility charges should be discussed in detail. The meeting manager should have a way of checking actual usage of the meeting area, and not use an average for all meeting space. Many locations will charge an average rate per hour, resulting in a meeting that uses a smaller amount of power subsidizing the big users.

For direct-charge contracts, it must be determined when the power (light, heat, and/or air-conditioning) will be turned on and when it will go off. If the power is turned on and off, will charges be made for each adjustment?

## INFORMATION SHEETS AND ACTIVITIES LIST

The meeting manager should request a copy of all internal correspondence concerning the meeting. These should be checked in detail. Errors and mistakes do happen. By checking all this information before the meeting, many problems can be avoided. This is a good give point for the location, since it really costs nothing.

## TABLE SIZES

Large facilities usually have several different sizes of table and the meeting manager should receive written assurance that the correct size will be provided for the meeting.

## HALL CONTROL AND SECURITY

Will areas outside the meeting room be shared with others? If so, will the meeting manager have any control over the movement of people not connected with the meeting in those areas? Can a special traffic pattern be set up for your meeting? Will the meeting manager have to assume any responsibility? Today security costs can be very high, especially for off-hours work.

## MEETING-ROOM SECURITY

The security of the meeting room is a major issue. For the meeting manager, it should be an issue on which there is no compromise. Today the cost of equipment can be very high for a meeting of average size. Any equipment that is lost is costly and could easily affect the objectives of the meeting.

## MEETING-ROOM TEMPERATURE

A problem that always seems insoluble is meeting-room temperature. The perfect temperature has not yet been found. At any temperature someone will not be happy. Who controls the temperature is an important issue.

## MATERIAL STORAGE

Today there are very few locations that will allow materials to be stored in the meeting room, mainly because of security considerations. The meeting manager must determine how much space will be needed, before the negotiations. The required security of storage rooms also should be determined. The meeting manager must also assure that if any large equipment is anticipated it can be moved from receiving to storage and then moved to the meeting room. Costs can be significant; if material must be moved any distance, with a big crew, the meeting manager may have a large bill.

## BREAKOUT ROOMS

Many training courses and conferences require small breakout rooms in which subgroups can meet for group projects, role-playing, and so forth. In negotiation courses, for example, such rooms would be needed so that both sides could plan a mock negotiation in privacy. The rates for the meeting room and breakout rooms may be different and are very negotiable.

## GROSS SPACE

One possibility is to negotiate a total square-foot package. It may be that this is cheaper, for the meeting manager, than paying on a room-by-room basis.

## CEILING HEIGHT

If any audiovisual aids will be used, ceiling height is critical. The ceiling must be high enough to allow the projection, especially if it is over a long distance.

## SERVICES—EXCLUSIVE USE

At some locations all service contracts are on an exclusive basis. That is, only one caterer, for example, has a contract with that location. If the meeting manager wants another caterer, the manager must "buy out" the exclusive caterer. That is, the manager will have to negotiate an agreement to use another caterer and pay for that right. The minimum that the caterer will ask for is a payment equal to gross profit. This issue may be very important if the group is an executive or sophisticated one.

## LIABILITY INSURANCE

At the start, most contracts state that the meeting manager is completely responsible for all damages. This is just a starting point. Contracts can be rewritten; words, sentences, paragraphs, and so forth can be crossed out and initaled. Because of the potential risk, it is advisable to have a lawyer review this section before the contract is signed.

## FIRE AND SAFETY LAWS

Most contracts will state that everything must conform to local laws. Before the meeting manager signs, he or she must find out what the laws are, whose regulations apply, which political organization has control, and so forth. Again, the potential risk is very high and the cost of liability could be very high.

## HEALTH AND SICKNESS

Do local laws require that a doctor and/or nurse be on duty at all times? This is an important question. Many trade shows will expect tens of thousands of visitors. The possibility that someone will have a health problem is very real. If no law applies, the meeting manager may decide to have a nurse as a minimum protection. This may help to reduce negligence suits in the future if someone gets sick. At a minimum, the manager should have a list of local doctors, dentists, and so forth who are very close to the location and will see people in the group on a priority basis.

## PARKING

If there is not enough parking space at the meeting location, what arrangements are available? Many motels have special low-cost arrangements with bus companies for shuttle service. The price of this should be negotiated. The meeting manager should ask why the guests should have to pay when they can park free at many locations. If there is enough parking, what does it cost? The meeting manager should also negotiate this cost.

## AUDIOVISUAL EQUIPMENT

If audiovisual equipment is required, the meeting manager must have a written guarantee that the equipment will be available. If an outside service provides this equipment, the manager should ask whether the hotel adds an overhead percentage. If so, this is negotiable.

## LIGHTING AND ELECTRICAL OUTLETS

The meeting manager should know of the location of light switches and electrical outlets. Are there enough outlets, and will they carry the load? If not, what alternatives are there, and who will pay?

## PERSONNEL

Two major aspects of personnel should be discussed: first, the types of skills the location will provide on a no-fee basis, and second, how flexible these people are.

## CLEANUP AFTER THE MEETING

Determining who is responsible for cleanup after the meeting is an important issue. Many a meeting manager has received a surprise when a bill arrived for cleanup costs. This could include moving the garbage to the collection point, or special collections. In some locations the local garbage collectors will only pick up certain types of material on their regular collection trips. A special fee is charged for "other materials." Many areas will not allow materials to be put out until collection day, so where it will be held is another consideration. A meeting that includes booths, exhibits, and so forth may have a lot of materials to be removed.

## CLEANUP DURING THE MEETING

Who will clean up during the meeting and how often is important. It makes a very poor impression when people sit down to tables that have half-empty glasses, full ash trays, and so forth. The property manager has responsibility for cleanup during the meeting. How well it is done is an area the meeting manager must address early. This is more than just a service.

## ACCESS TO HOTEL AND ROOM

If the meeting manager anticipates any large equipment, access to the property is important. The maximum height and width dimensions for all possible entrance points must be determined. This information should be given to all possible exhibitors so that they do not find out the hard way that their booth equipment, and so forth will not fit. All possible access points should be discussed. If the meeting manager negotiates at the location, he or she can see all areas that will affect the meeting.

## ADVERTISEMENTS

Many locations have large signboards outside. This is a way to advertise certain groups. A good give point for the property is to use the signboard. Printed advertising is another possibility.

The meeting manager should push such advertisements. It can be important to private businesses. They can have their names put in front of potential customers at a very low cost or no cost.

## INTERIOR SIGNS

Where the meeting manager can put directional signs and advertising signs inside the location is another point. Who is authorized to put up signs and whether there are any size limitations should also be discussed.

## BREAKS

The how, where, when, and so forth of breaks must be determined. Breaks must be on time or the meeting will fall behind. The location is also important.

## MEAL MENUS

Meal menus could be a no-win situation similar to meeting-room temperature. Someone will find fault with any selection. The a la carte prices should be compared with prices for complete meals. It may be cheaper to have less, especially at lunch, on an item-by-item basis. Whether the hotel can provide special meals (salt-free, for example), and what they cost, is also an item for the negotiation agenda.

## HOSPITALITY ROOM

The cost of a hospitality room is very negotiable. If the meeting is large, more than one room or a suite of rooms may be required, and should be free.

## HOSPITALITY ROOM STOCKING

Stocking the hospitality room has an important impact on cost. If the manager must buy all liquor, mixes, and so forth from the hotel, the cost will be more than twice the cost of buying these items outside. This is negotiable. Many locations will allow meeting managers to bring in their own liquor.

## FREE (COMP) ROOMS

The meeting manager should take the position that for every $x$ number of paid rooms, one free (comp) room should be provided. The manager will want to establish the concept long before the exact percentage is negotiated. For the property manager this means a direct reduction of profit. Giving on this issue will have to be offset with getting something else.

## ROOMING LISTS AND CHECK-IN PROCEDURE

Preregistered check-in is a nice touch for meeting guests. It saves time for both the guest and for the location. A win-win situation can be developed here.

## ROOM ASSIGNMENTS

Most hotels will try to assign rooms for all members of a group in the same area of the hotel. There are many positive reasons for this: group members do not bother other guests, they can get together easily, the hospitality room is close. The meeting manager, however, cannot assume this will happen automatically this service must be negotiated.

## AIRPORT LIMOUSINE SERVICE

Getting to and from the airport can be problem. For a big meeting, the meeting manager should start by asking for free limousine service and negotiate from there.

## MEETING AGENDA CONFIRMATION

The hotel must ask for copies of the meeting or training course agenda. This is their double check that no errors were made. (See the Information Sheets and Activities List subheading.)

## ASSIGNMENT SHEET COPIES

Copies of assignment sheets are given to hotel employees by the hotel management. The meeting manager should also have these so that he or she can directly contact the correct person if a problem arises.

## SIGNATURE AUTHORITY

Who can sign for charges to the company or organization conducting the meeting is critical. This authorization must be in writing and clearly understood by both sides.

## BILLINGS—MASTER VERSUS INDIVIDUAL

Which charges will be made to the individual participant and which charges will go on the organization's account (master) must be in writing—item-by-item.

## LATE CHECKOUTS

For a large meeting late checkouts could be a problem. The manager should negotiate for this ahead of time even if he or she does not know who will want a late checkout. One suggestion is to negotiate a percentage of rooms to be allowed a late checkout. Then the meeting manager controls the list during the meeting.

## BAGGAGE STORAGE

In many hotels there is a per-bag charge for storage.This is negotiable. A motel will generally not risk losing a big meeting just to get $.25 per bag in its storage room.

## MINIMUM ROOMS AND MEALS GUARANTEE

An important point for the hotel is to obtain, in writing, a guarantee for a minimum number of rooms and a minimum number at each meal. The hotel cannot assume that the expected number of people will show up. If the manager wants rooms reserved, the hotel cannot be expected to reserve them until the last minute and have them be empty.

## PAYMENT SCHEDULE

The location manager should start with the position that money must be paid up front, for example 25 percent upon signing the contract, 50 percent one month before the meeting, and the balance at the end of the meeting. The meeting manager's initial position should be to pay everything after the meeting, or perhaps everything less retainage. Whatever, is agreed to, this point is very important with today's high interest rates.

## TOTAL PRICE

Total price must be determined. It is important for the property manager so he or she knows the value of the meeting. It is important for the meeting manager so that a comparison with other locations can be made.

## KEY CONTACTS—MEETING MANAGER

The location manager should insist that only one person be the official contact for the meeting. It is impossible if several people associated with the meeting, try to tell the location manager to do something. Many times the "somethings" may be very different.

## KEY CONTACTS—LOCATION DAY AND NIGHT

As a corollary, the meeting manager must have a single contact at the location who will handle all problems not resolved at a lower level.

## MAINTENANCE SUPERVISOR MEETING

A good practice for a meeting manager is to require a meeting with the maintenance supervisor. First, any special problems can be solved before the business meeting. Second, this will open communications so that problems during the meeting can be solved quickly.

## AUDIT PROCEDURES

After the meeting, an audit must be completed to assure that all charges are valid. Since problems may happen, the audit procedure should be determined before the meeting. The audit should take place as soon as possible and a system to resolve conflicts established. This is in the best interests of both sides.

## CREDIT AUTHORITY

The hotel should check credit ratings of the company or organization before the final contract is signed. Poor credit risks should pay more.

## OTHER MEETINGS

Most meetings are not one-shot deals. In the training area, many courses are given each year. Most meetings or conferences meet every year. Future business is most important. Depending upon the level of business, it may be more important to the seller or the buyer. It can be a major influence in the negotiations.

## ASSISTANCE WITH PLANNED RECREATION

If there will be planned activities (e.g., golf, tennis, fishing, tours, etc.), the location can provide valuable assistance. The cost is negotiable.

As with other negotiations these issues are just the start. For your special situation add more to your list below:

1. _____
2. _____
3. _____
4. _____
5. _____
6. _____
7. _____
8. _____
9. _____
10. _____

# CHAPTER 9

# Issues in Other Negotiations

The last four chapters have covered a minimum number of issues to be considered during the planning for buyer-seller, management-labor, business, or conference negotiations. These lists are starting points for planning for negotiations. Many other issues should be considered for each particular negotiation, since each negotiation is unique. The more issues considered, the greater is the probability of success.

This is also true of the other types of negotiations. Sooner or later just about everyone in our society buys a car. The car buyer is usually at a distinct disadvantage. First, the buyer may not know as much as the seller about all the technical areas of buying and selling cars. Not very many people are automobile mechanics or engineers. The seller will usually know more about the automobile. The seller also knows more about the marketplace. Third, and very important, the seller has much more experience negotiating. Today most people are planning to buy a car every four to six years. The seller may negotiate four times a day. This works out to 1,000 times per year. If you buy a car once every five years, the seller will have had approximately 5,000 negotiations since your last automobile negotiation. This is a major advantage. Because of this, planning for an automobile purchase should be very detailed. List all the important issues before you start visiting the dealers. You should be able to develop a list of many issues.

Another item to be considered when buying an automobile is that the buyer is both the agent and principal. In approximately 95 perent of all business negotiations the negotiator is an agent; the negotiator represents and works for the business, the company, union, and so forth. When you are in that position you are able to focus on doing the best negotiating job. You should be able to avoid deep emotional involvement. That is a problem when you are both agent and principal, however. The principal part of you could become involved and not do the best negotiating job. Countless times a husband and wife have lost an automobile negotiation because of their preferences—the color, the racing stripes, and so forth. They "had" to have a certain car and in all probability paid too much. On the sales side of this type of negotiation the salesperson is an agent. Very seldom do you negotiate with the owner. The seller can be more objective, rational, and so forth, and this is a major advantage.

The largest negotiation that most of us enter into as an individual is buying or selling a house. This always has a major impact on the financial success of both families. Again, we generally act as both agent and principal. There is usually a real estate specialist who is more of a consultant or adviser than the chief negotiator. Often the agent represents both sides and serves as a go-between and technical expert. Because of the magnitude of this type of negotiation, a well-developed list of issues must be developed before any negotiation is started.

As we review our lives we can think of many other types of negotiations we have or will be involved in. For each, a detailed list of issues should be developed before the negotiation starts. It cannot be emphasized too strongly or too often that the side that is most prepared usually wins a negotiation. Preparation includes considering every issue that could be discussed in the negotiation. If one side is prepared on any issue and the other side is not prepared, the prepared side will generally win that issue.

We even could negotiate as an agent for our country. These negotiations will follow a very firm planning process. Many books have been written about negotiations between nations, so it will not be reviewed here.

As a starting point, the major issues to be considered in two of the most important negotiations that we participate in as individuals—buying a house and buying a car—are listed. As in the last four chapters, the issues are not listed in priority order, but they are grouped. For each negotiation the priority of the issues will be different. You must evaluate each negotiation separately.

## ISSUES TO BE CONSIDERED WHEN BUYING OR SELLING A HOUSE

### Neighborhood

It is essential that the buyer meet and talk to some of the neighbors before making a buying decision. Items to consider are their ages, interests, children, time schedules, hobbies, involvement in the community, and so forth.

### Easements

Easements refer to a third-party's rights of access to the land. A good example is a utility easement. For example, one couple almost purchased a house with a major easement before they found out about it. More than 50 percent of the land (70 of 122 feet) was covered by a utility easement. They could not do anything with this land—that they would own and pay taxes on—because of the easement.

### Quality of Water

Thousands of areas have slightly contaminated water. A buyer must check out the quality of the water supply. If there is a well, a smart buyer will check with the neighbor before buying.

## Public Transportation

Even if you have several cars, public transportation is very important. It is possible that all the cars will need to be repaired at the same time and public transportation will be the only available way to get around. Aspects of public transportation to consider include:

Routes

Schedule

Vehicles

Costs

Stop locations

Safety record

## Severe Weather Possibilities

It is not smart to purchase a house on a major earthquake fault line, or in an area that floods every year, or in an area with a probability of hurricanes, and so forth. Much research should be completed before purchase. Even if you can buy insurance, it will never replace your family keepsakes or special mementos.

## Public Schools (Grammar, Middle, High)

If you have school-age children, public schools are critical. If you do not have children, or the children are grown, this issue is still very important because it will affect the resale value of the house. Aspects of public schools to consider include:

Distance to public schools

Major roads that must be crossed

Time schedule at school

Athletic opportunities

Cultural opportunities

Civic opportunities

Music opportunities

Fine arts opportunities

History of safety at school

Percentage of students who go on to higher education

Trend of school enrollments

Other opportunities at school

## Resale Value

Many factors determine resale value. It is most important. Sooner or later the house will be sold. Even if you keep it until you die, resale value will be important, especially for your heirs. If you sell before you die, it will be a major factor. In every city of the world, the value of houses appreciate better in some sections than in others.

## Utility Costs

The buyer must ask for the last three years of costs for all utilities (gas, electricity, water, sewers, etc.) and evaluate these numbers. If one of these years has been abnormal (very cold, very hot, very wet, etc.), then the buyer must get four years of data. If the seller will not provide the information, it may be available from the local utilities.

## Age of All Appliances

If appliances are included in the sale, it is very important to obtain the ages of each appliance. The buyer should also check with service companies to determine at which age each appliance has trouble. You want to avoid the problems of one couple who purchased a house with appliances and had to buy four new ones in less than a year. All four items "died." This couple lost money because the house did not really sell with "all appliances."

## Roof

Before you even consider buying a house, the condition of the roof *must* be considered.

## Zoning

The zoning of the immediate area, as well as that several blocks away, must be checked. It is possible that a business or commercial complex a few blocks away could lower the value of a house, especially if built after the house was purchased.

## Regional Development Considerations

A wise buyer will check with area development commissions to review their future plans and how these plans could affect the value of the house.

## Insulation

Recently, several insulation materials have been found to have toxic components that are very dangerous. A buyer must assure that he or she knows what materials have been used and that these materials are safe.

## Flight Path for Local Airport

The day that a potential buyer visits a house that is for sale may be a day when all the flights are landing or taking off in an opposite direction. After the person buys and moves in, airplanes could be flying right over the house 90 percent of the time. Be sure to ask.

## Taxes

Many different items will affect the total taxes paid. It is most important that the buyer determine the total tax obligation. One factor (mileage rate, for example) may be low in one area, but the other components (assessed value) may be very high. The net cost is the only important item.

Assessed value
Mile rate

Cap for maximum taxes

Cap for increase per year

Frequency of reassessments

Relationship of price to assessed value

Process for changing mile rate

Process for changing assessed value

## Commuting Time to Work Location

Commuting time in both mornings and evenings must be considered. It is possible that because of staggered times one commuting period (A.M. or P.M.) is free of problems, while the other period has many problems. A smart buyer will actually drive to work from a potential house at rush hour, both mornings and evenings.

## Sprinkler Systems

In many areas automatic sprinkler systems are installed under grass and/or shrub areas. The condition, cost, and so forth of such systems should be reviewed.

## Age of Home

Fifteen years is a major point in a house's life. After this time, the buyer must expect problems.

## Cost of Insurance

This is a function of replacement value and insurance rates.

## Affordability of Loan

The usual standard for determining whether someone can afford a loan is 33 percent of gross salary for housing costs. A very conservative bank will only lend up to 20 percent and a very liberal bank will go up to 40 percent.

## Sales Expenses

In many areas past precedents have established that the buyer or the seller will pay certain sales expenses. This does not mean that they cannot be negotiated. Each of the following can and should be negotiated. If a law requires that one side pays a certain item, it can still be negotiated and the value of the item used to adjust the final price.

State transfer tax

County transfer tax

Local transfer tax

Attorneys' fees

Broker's commission

Title search

Title abstract

Title insurance

Survey costs

Mortgage prepayment penalty

Mortgage satisfaction fee

Credit report

Mortgage service charge

Recording fees

Miscellaneous settlement costs

Mortgage appraisal fee

Finder's fee

Placement fees

Buyer's mortgage discount points

Listing costs

Escrow costs

Tax escrow accounts

Insurance escrow accounts

Utility escrow accounts

Utility cutoff/connection dates

Utility cutoff/connection costs

Interest earned on escrow accounts

Interest earned on deposits

Interest earned on good faith money

Utility deposits

Special assessments

Security deposits

Continuation of abstract of title

Cost of preparation of settlement papers

Cost for closing agent

Capital gains tax

State income tax (gains)

Local income tax (gains)

Mortgage insurance costs

Miscellaneous carrying costs

Mobil home hook-up costs

Mobile home land lease costs

Mobile home tax proration

## Other Factors

The following additional factors in buying or selling a house are essentially self-explanatory

1.  Size of rooms
    a.  Living room
    b.  Dining room
    c.  Den
    d.  Kitchen
    e.  Master bedroom
    f.  Other bedrooms
    g.  Bathrooms

    h. Laundry room

    i. Basement

    j. Attic

    k. Garage

2. Total square footage of house

3. Pool and/or hot tub

    a. Size

    b. Water pump system

    c. Water filter system

    d. Water heating system

    e. Pool accessories

    f. Pool insurance

    g. Pool protection

    h. Winter pool care

    i. Costs to maintain pool at various water temperatures

4. Security systems

5. Storage space

6. Size of closets

7. Lot size

    a. Livable space

    b. Garden space

    c. Entertaining space

    d. Room for expansion

    e. Distance from house to lot line

8. Landscaping/age of trees and shrubs

9. Business contacts nearby

10. Church locations

11. Shopping center locations

12. Restaurant locations

13. Recreation locations

    a. Golf

    b. Tennis

    c.   Spa/Health club

    d.   Swimming pool

    e.   "Sandlot" fields

    f.   Fishing

    g.   Organized team sports

    h.   Professional team sports

**14.** Cultural locations

**15.** Views

**16.** Automobile service center locations

**17.** Accessibility to major highways

**18.** Accessibility to major airports

**19.** Type of heating system

**20.** Prepurchase inspections

    a.   Heating/cooling system

    b.   Electrical system

    c.   Water pipes

    d.   Roof

    e.   Pool/hot tub

    f.   Termites

    g.   Security system

**21.** Perception of value versus location

**22.** Air pollution considerations

**23.** Average weather conditions—winter/summer

    a.   Temperature

    b.   Rain/snowfall

    c.   Windspeed

    d.   Maximum extreme conditions

**24.** Condominiums versus houses

**25.** Location of medical facilities

**26.** Laundry room location (inside or outside)

**27.** Price

**28.** Mortgage rate

29. Mortgage time
30. Mortgage producer
31. Second mortgages
32. Assumability of current mortgage
33. Down payment
34. Blueprints/plans/drawings
35. Assessments (current/future)
36. Alternate commuting routes
37. Type of air-conditioning system
38. College and university locations

Here is an area to list special points of individual interest to each reader.

1. _____
2. _____
3. _____
4. _____
5. _____
6. _____
7. _____
8. _____
9. _____
10. _____

## ISSUES TO BE CONSIDERED WHEN BUYING A CAR

### Mileage

If the car has been previously owned, be sure to get a certificate of mileage. Also, check the speedometer to see if it has been tampered with.

## Undercoating

Undercoating is negotiable and many times a dealer will provide it free in order to make a sale.

## Options

Generally, the dealer makes a significant margin on all options added to the base car. This margin is a good area for the buyer to attack during the negotiations. The buyer should not indicate a need for the option, only an interest. If the seller determines that any item is a requirement for the buyer, the seller will have no incentive to negotiate. A few examples are:

Radio
FM radio
Cassette tape/radio
Radio with citizen's band
Rear speakers
Air-conditioning
Special wheel covers
Special paint
Positive traction rear end.
More powerful engine
Rear window defroster
Electric windows
Electric seats
Electrically controlled outside mirrors
Power radio antenna

## Legal Costs

In many states sales taxes must be paid on the purchase of a car. This could be five to seven percent of the final price. If a buyer can negotiate an agreement with the seller to split the tax cost, the buyer will save considerably. When the seller says it is impossible for two to pay a tax, all the buyer has to counter with is that the seller can simply reduce the price by that amount. (When this happens, the buyer will get a second savings since his or her half of the tax will be on a lower figure.)

The costs to prepare a title, to register a car, and so forth are other points to be negotiated. At the prices of today's cars, every dollar saved by the buyer (or gained by the seller) is important.

Taxes

Title

Registration

License plates

Inspection sticker

Smog control inspection

## Day of the Month

Car sales are reported in 10-day periods. The last day of each period is a good time to negotiate a new car purchase. The dealer and/or the salesperson may need just one more sale to make the quota for the period. It is very possible they will sell that car at a low price. It is possible that they would give up a margin or commission to reach the objective and obtain a bonus.

## Deal with Decision Maker

How many times has a car buyer had the following experience?

SALESPERSON:   "Reviewing these numbers then, do we have a deal?"

BUYER:   "Yes, we have a deal."

SALESPERSON:   "Let me get my sales manager's approval."

During the five-minute wait, the buyer sees himself or herself in the car, driving down the road, has made the financial decision, and is emotionally committed.

The seller returns and says, "The boss wouldn't buy the deal.

You'll have to pay another $100" (generally because the trade-in value of the old car was too high or because an option was not priced correctly). Since the buyer has already "purchased" the car, what is another $100 he or she thinks, so the buyer agrees.

This issue is very important. Buyers should only negotiate with a person who can make a firm commitment. The buyer should ask first about authority limits. The $100 is only a small part of the price of a new car, maybe one percent. But if this happens on every sale of 10 million cars, the extra income to sellers is one billion dollars.

## Extras/Renewal Parts

During the life of a car, the owner will have to replace many items. For every 30,000 miles there will be one set of tires, four oil filters, four oil changes, four air filters, one set of fan belts, and so forth. Before the purchase commitment, the buyer should ask for some or all of these items. To start, the buyer should ask for these free of charge but may have to agree to pay factory cost to make the deal. The seller may need to make a sale and will agree to selling the extras at no margin or profit.

## Extras/Special Parts

In some areas snow tires are a necessity. An extra set of rims and snow tires should be included in the purchase. Again, the buyer's initial position should be to request these to be free, with a fall-back position to offering to pay factory cost. Another example of this is a child's safety seat.

## Extras/Dealer Costs

Several items are included here. Each can be negotiated. They generally are charged at a standard rate that may not have a direct relationship to cost. A buyer should investigate all areas.

Dealer preparation
Transportation
Loading/unloading
Paperwork preparation

## Financing Charges

All loans are not the same. The rate can vary. The dealer may want to finance through his or her own financing institution. These rates may be higher than a local bank or savings and loan. A buyer should ask for and get rates from several money sources. If the dealer has financing, the rate is open for negotiation. When interest rates are in the 10–15 percent range, the cost of money is a major expense for the buyer, which the buyer must negotiate.

## Financing Commission

In some cases, the seller and/or the dealer may receive a commission for selling a loan. If so, this is a good area for a buyer to negotiate. The seller may be willing to take less commission on the loan in order to sell a car and assure some commission for selling the car.

## After-Sale Service

During the life of a car, routine service will be required many times. It is also quite possible that defects will have to be repaired. Some manufacturers and dealers offer a maintenance plan (e.g., a "buyer protection plan") to reduce the buyer's risk. The cost of this plan is very negotiable. The base of any such plan is future risk. This is an unknown factor for any one car. The average risk is known, but that has little relevance to any one sale. In order to make a sale (especially if it is a buyer's condition of purchase), the dealer may provide a protection plan at no cost, or reduced cost.

The buyer should also discuss a discount for routine service. This issue is a good example of an issue that can be very valuable to a buyer. Before a sale, a seller may be willing to negotiate, but after the sale the buyer has absolutely no leverage.

## Inventory Costs

Experts generally estimate the cost of carrying inventory as between 20 and 33 percent per year of the value of the item. Each day that a car stays in inventory (on the lot) is an expense to the dealer. Inventory cost includes items such as: cost of money, cost of space, cost of handling, cost of maintaining records, and so forth. Buyers should use this point in negotiations. The savings to the dealer of reducing inventory costs is negotiable.

### Buyer's Need

Whenever possible, a buyer should negotiate to buy a car when the buyer does not need a new (or newer) car. If the buyer must buy, he or she is in a weak position. The seller has significantly less incentive to negotiate.

Two examples will show different types of need. In many states annual or semiannual inspections are required. If a buyer starts to look for a new car because the current car will not pass inspection (or will cost a lot to repair) a few days before the inspection date, the buyer is in a very weak position. The seller will realize that a buy must be made and will not give as much.

The second example involves a special feature (e.g., a three-way tailgate on a stationwagon). If the buyer lets the seller know that he or she really wants this feature, the seller has no reason to negotiate.

### Value of Trade-In to Dealer/to Private Individual

The value of a trade-in is an area in which most sellers should have a major advantage. The real value of the car is a most important point. Buyers must do a lot of research to try to determine the current value of their cars. There are publications that can be purchased that list the value of cars ("blue book value"), but these may not be true for your specific area or the actual time of year. If possible, a buyer should try to get the actual price paid for recent sales in the buyer's area.

In summary buying a car or buying a house is very important to most of us. We must do as much planning for these negotiations as we do for any other negotiation. We must consider all the issues before the negotiation, if we expect to win the negotiation.

Here you can add your special auto items:

1. _____
2. _____
3. _____
4. _____
5. _____
6. _____
7. _____
8. _____
9. _____
10. _____

# Take Time to Plan

## TAKE TIME TO PLAN

It takes a lot of time to plan a negotiation. As you have read through and considered the checkpoints, ideas, charts, and issues of planning a negotiation in the first nine chapters, I hope that you have gained an appreciation of the magnitude of good negotiation planning.

The negotiator must start the planning process far enough in advance to that he or she is fully prepared on the day negotiations start. You should consider postponing the negotiation if you are not ready, unless there is a legal requirement that prevents postponement. Every negotiator agrees that it takes longer to plan than they anticipated. Problems can occur during the planning stage: An important document is lost, a "fire drill" is called in your area of responsibility, a person is promoted, and so forth. If you believe that it will take 13 hours to plan, allow at least 39 hours. If you believe that it will take one week to plan, allow at least 10 working days.

If you cannot postpone the negotiation, use delaying tactics during the negotiation session and finish your planning outside the negotiation room. When you are fully prepared, then you can get serious in the negotiation.

An important consideration in deciding how much time to devote to planning is how much you could gain from the negotiation. This is the return-on-investment concept (ROI (return on investment) = SAVINGS ÷ INVESTMENT). Several examples will illustrate this concept. First, you are a buyer and have an order to place for 10 boxes of pencils whose total value is $27. The maximum that could be saved might be $7, so you will only be able to invest 20–30 minutes to do your planning. Second, you are a labor negotiator negotiating a contract for 100,000 workers whose annual wages are $22,700 per person (total of $2.27 billion). The gain per each one percent raise is over $20 million. In this case, a year's planning would be well worth the time invested.

Each negotiator must also understand that the first time he or she completes the planning process, it will take longer than the second time. The learning curve concept also applies to negotiation planning. This is especially true for the second time you plan the same negotiation. Many items will only have to be updated the second time around. The MAP form must be retained after the negotiation. These make for a very good history of the item negotiated. Also they are excellent for training a new person taking over responsibility for the item. This should significantly reduce training time.

Figures 10-1 and 10-2 show examples of a MAP form with headings and a form with all lines filled in. This is an example of how your form will look. I cannot encourage you enough to use this process for your next important negotiation. It will take a little extra work, but the investment will be worth it.

Once you understand the planning process, you can adapt it to your specific negotiations. Using the example of the pencil buyer, with an understanding of the planning process, the buyer could complete a shortened MAP form, perhaps on scratch paper, just before the buyer makes the call to order the pencils. This would prepare the buyer and help assure the maximum possible savings on the purchase.

This chapter is just a reminder to start your planning far enough in advance of the start of negotiations. Then you will be fully pre-

| Position | | | | | | | Signature | | | | | | | | |
|---|---|---|---|---|---|---|---|---|---|---|---|---|---|---|---|
| ① | ② | ③ | ④ | ⑤ | ⑥ | ⑦ | ⑧ | ⑨ | ⑩ | ⑪ | ⑫ | ⑬ | ⑭ | ⑮ | ⑯ |
| Issues | Type | $V_M$ | $V_{MR}$ | $V_{OR}$ | $V_O$ | Authority Limit | Information | Agenda | $IP_M$ | $O_M$ | $O_O$ | $IP_O$ | Tactics | Results | Delta |
| Avoid Issues | | | | | | | | | | | | | | | |

**FIGURE 10-1** MAP

Strong / Position

*a. M. Boss* — Signature

| | (1) Issues | (2) Type | (3) $V_M$ | (4) $V_{MR}$ | (5) $V_{OR}$ | (6) $V_O$ | (7) Authority Limit | (8) Information | (9) Agenda | (10) $IP_M$ | (11) $O_M$ | (12) $O_O$ | (13) $IP_O$ | (14) Tactics | (15) Results | (16) Delta |
|---|---|---|---|---|---|---|---|---|---|---|---|---|---|---|---|---|
| Cash Terms | | W | 1% = $2,700 | — | — | 1% = $2,700 | Net 30 days | 2 | 3 | 3% in 30 days | 2% in 15 days | 1% in 10 days | Net in 30 days | Lower than the boss | 2% in 10 days | $51 per year |
| Avoid Issues / Lead Time | | — | $5,000/week | | | $10,000/week | Max 13 weeks | 7 | — | — | — | 13 weeks | 27 weeks | — | X | X |

FIGURE 10-2 MAP

pared. It is a superior feeling to walk into a negotiation's room fully prepared and completely confident that you will do an outstanding job. In that case you just can't wait to get started. When you do start, the results will be the best possible for you, the negotiator, and your principal, if there is one.

# CHAPTER 11

# Summary

One of the first reactions that students in my seminars have, after reviewing the negotiation planning process, is that it is too detailed. They say it is not necessary to complete *all* the steps in the checklist, to review *all* the points to be negotiated, to do *all* this planning, that they can do a good job without *all* this work. This just is not true. In the real world, many negotiations are lost because of poor planning, especially because of failure to consider all the issues to be negotiated.

Consider this example of a situation that actually happened. One company was negotiating to purchase a small company. The larger company had gross sales billed that were at least 30 times larger than those of the smaller company. The larger company had very experienced people as compared with those in the smaller company. The purchase was a friendly one. Both sides wanted the deal. The only area to negotiate was the terms of purchase. A deal was negotiated, the larger company bought the small company, and made a small company division. As the assimilation process was taking place, it became apparent that the building that housed the manufacturing area needed to be changed. At that point, the larger company "discovered" that the purchase did not include the buildings. The larger company had to spend more money to buy the buildings. It assumed it had bought the buildings. It happened because the larger company did not do a complete job of planning. It cannot be emphasized too strongly how important planning is in every negotiation.

Another example concerns a consultant. The consultant developed a special seminar in negotiations for purchasing in bad business conditions. The first seminar was presented late in 1980. The pilot seminar received extremely high ratings. The ratings were higher than expected, higher than most other public seminars usually given, so a decision was made to present another seminar in 1981.

Based upon the fact that all went well with the first seminar, the consultant made a major mistake and trusted the seminar sponsor. The consultant believed that he did not have to protect himself. He did not even ask about terms for the second seminar and just scheduled the date on his calendar.

After the seminar, held in April 1981, an expense report and invoice were sent to the sponsor. (All expenses had been paid by the consultant.) Because the consultant trusted the sponsor and had not established a firm payment date, the sponsor decided it did not have to pay until it was good and ready to do so.

The consultant waited patiently for payment because he understood that it takes a while for larger companies to process paperwork. A three-month wait was not unusual. In August, four months later, he decided to check into his pay. Remember, all the expenses were out of his pocket, so he not only did not get paid, but he had in fact underwritten the seminar. The sponsor was working with his money. Since the prime rate at the time was about 18 percent, the sponsor was making $1\frac{1}{2}$ percent per month on his money. The consultant called his contact at the sponsoring company only to discover that she was not available.

During the period of August to December, 1981, he called at least once a week, but no one would talk to him. Most of the time he was never allowed to talk to anyone because the telephone operator just took a message.

During this time he had not been paid and did not know when he would be paid. It seemed as if the sponsor did not care whether the consultant was ever paid. Although the consultant taught a negotiations seminar, he did not negotiate *his own* contract very well because he did not cover all the points to be negotiated (i.e., terms of payment). Only after the consultant retained a lawyer did he get paid.

A book could be filled with similar examples. The point of reviewing these two examples is to reinforce the importance of the planning process reviewed in this book. In the real world, thousands of people are negotiating every day, and most of these people are not very successful because they do not do a complete planning job. They do not cover all the issues, checkpoints, and ideas presented in this book. They do not invest the time. They do not believe it is necessary.

Planning will typically take more effort than the actual negotiation and will vary in time based upon the importance of the negotiation, but it is essential. Since negotiations are just the start of a longer relationship, all of the conflict in the world today (buyer-seller, company-company, nation-nation, husband-wife, parent-child, etc.) indicates that many past negotiations have not been very successful.

This book contains three major elements to help you plan negotiations:

1.  A 25-point checklist of activities that must be completed before starting a negotiation.
2.  An MAP form that can be used to organize all the information so that it can be used as effectively as possible.
3.  A listing of all the issues to be considered in the planning stage of various types of negotiations.

The underlying concept of this book is that if one side is prepared to negotiate an issue in any negotiation and the opponent is not prepared, the prepared side will win that issue. A very detailed step-by-step process will assure that nothing is overlooked.

In most negotiations the side that is best prepared is the side that obtains its objectives in the negotiation. This book will assure that if you complete the process, you will be the most prepared and achieve your objectives.

CHAPTER 12

# Reading Library

Many books have been written about negotiations. In this chapter 24 books specifically addressing negotiation and 33 closely related books are listed. All of these address the psychology of the process and/or the actual process (strategies, tactics, dos, don'ts, etc.). This book is the the only that addresses the planning part of negotiations. After it is read, it can continue to be used as a reference.

In Chapter 1 it was discussed that the material in this book would be presented similar to a live seminar. At the end of each negotiation's seminar the following library list is passed out. It is not complete, but it is a start.

For you to become a real expert in negotiations, you are urged to regularly study the subject. Set an objective of one new book per month. Each book has valuable information and points to improve your negotiation results.

This book should be the keystone of your library, since planning is the key to success. The other books will provide information in other areas of negotiations. This book will assure that you have a process to improve your planning for future negotiations, so that you can "talk for money" more effectively.

## NEGOTIATION BOOKS

1. *Negotiate the Deal You Want*—Calero and Oskam (Dodd, Mead) 1983
2. *Winning the Negotiation*—Calero (Hawthorn), 1979
3. *The Negotiating Game*—Karrass (World), 1970
4. *Give and Take*—Karrass (Crowell), 1974
5. *Sales Negotiation Strategies*—Hanan (AMA), 1977
6. *Negotiated Procurement Techniques*—Mitchell (AMA), 1962
7. *Negotiated Purchasing*—DeRose (Materials Management Institute), 1962
8. *The Negotiator: A Manual for Winners*—Coffin (AMA), 1973
9. *The Anatomy of a Win*—Beveridge (Beveridge), 1964
10. *How Nations Negotiate*—Ikle (Harper & Row), 1964
11. *How to Negotiate A Successful Contract*—Brown (Prentice-Hall), 1955
12. *The Art of Negotiating*—Nierenberg (Hawthorn), 1968
13. *Creative Business Negotiating*—Nierenberg (Hawthorn), 1971
14. *You Can Negotiate Anything*—Cohen (McGraw-Hill), 1982
15. *Winning by Negotiation*—Warschew (McGraw-Hill), 1980

## RELATED TOPICS

1. *How to Read a Person Like a Book*—Calero and Nierenberg (Hawthorn), 1971
2. *Meta-Talk*—Calero and Nierenberg (Hawthorn), 1973
3. *Management Science*—Thompson (McGraw-Hill), 1976
4. *Winning Through Intimidation*—Ringer (LA Book Publishers), 1973
5. *Fights, Games and Debates*—Rapoport (University of Michigan Press), 1960
6. *Face to Face Communication*—Anastasi (Management Center of Cambridge), 1967
7. *Nonverbal Communication for Business Success*—Cooper (AMA), 1979
8. *The Time Trap*—MacKenzie (AMA), 1970
9. *Managers' Guide to Speaking and Listening*—Connelly (AMA), 1969
10. *Body Language*—Fast (Evans), 1970
11. *Getting Through to People*—Nierenberg (Prentice-Hall), 1968
12. *The Order of Presentation in Persuasion*—Howland (Yale University Press), 1957
13. *The Executive Jungle*—Rodman (Nash), 1972

14. *The Territorial Imperative*—Audrey (Dell), 1966
15. *Systems Contracting*—Bolton (AMA), 1966
16. *The Purchasing Agent's Guide to the Naked Salesman*—Hersker and Stroh (Cahners), 1975
17. *The Art of Argument*—Aubyn (Emerson), 1962
18. *The Art of Getting Your Own Sweet Way*—Crosby (McGraw-Hill), 1972
19. *PO: A Device for Successful Thinking*—de Bono (Simon & Schuster), 1972
20. *Conceptual Blockbusting*—Adams (Norton), 1974
21. *Take the Road to Creativity*—Campbell (Argus), 1977

## GOVERNMENT-ORIENTED BOOKS

1. *Armed Services Procurement Manual for Contract Pricing*—(U.S. Government Printing Office), 1969
2. *Contracting with the Federal Government*—(Procurement), 1972
3. *Federal Procurement Law*—Nash and Cibinic (George Washington University Press), 1969
4. *Government Contracts Guide*—(Commerce Clearning House), 1972
5. *Handbook of Government Contract Administration*—Riemer (Prentice-Hall), 1968
6. *Improvement Curves*—(Procurement Associates), 1967
7. *Negotiation and Management of Defense Contracts*—Pace (Wiley), 1970
8. *Negotiation of Government Contracts*—McDonald (Procurement), 1972
9. *Negotiator's Handbook*—(Naval Material Command), 1958

## GENERAL TOPICS

1. *Megatrends*—Naisbitt (Warner Books), 1982
2. *In Search of Excellence*—Peters and Waterman (Harper & Row), 1982
3. *The Art of Japanese Management*—Athos and Pascale (Simon & Schuster), 1981
4. *The Third Wave*—Toffler (Morrow), 1980
5. *Marketing for Business Growth*—Levitt (McGraw-Hill), 1974
6. *The One Minute Manager*—Blanchard and Johnson (Morrow), 1982
7. *The Eastasia Edge*—Calder and Hufheinz (Basic), 1982
8. *Managing in Turbulent Times*—Drucker (Harper & Row), 1980
9. *Future Shock*—Toffler (Random House), 1970
10. *Material Requirements Planning*—Orlicky (McGraw-Hill), 1975
11. *Production and Inventory Control*—Plossl and Wight (Prentice-Hall), 1967
12. *Production and Inventory Management*—Fogarty and Hoffmann (South-Western), 1983

# Index